# STUDYING Gladiator
Sandy Irvine

## Contents

# Factsheet

| | |
|---|---|
| *Gladiator* | 2000, USA |
| Running time | 154 minutes |
| Certificate | 'R' in America and 15 in UK |
| Production company | DreamWorks SKG, Scott Free Productions and Universal Pictures |
| Distributor | Universal Pictures and, in some countries, United International Pictures |

## Key credits

| | |
|---|---|
| Director | Ridley Scott |
| Original story | David H. Franzoni |
| Screenplay | David H. Franzoni, John Logan and William Nicholson |
| Production designer | Arthur Max |
| Director of Photography | John Mathieson |
| Music | Hans Zimmer in collaboration with Lisa Gerrard |
| Editor | Pietro Scalia |
| Costume designer | Janty Yates |
| Budget | $103,000,000 (according to the Internet Movie Database) |

## Cast

| | |
|---|---|
| Maximus, a Roman general | Russell Crowe |
| Commodus, Emperor's son | Joaquin Phoenix |
| Lucilla, Emperor's daughter | Connie Nielson |
| Marcus Aurelius, Emperor of Rome | Richard Harris |
| Proximo, Gladiator 'entrepreneur' | Oliver Reed |
| Gracchus, Roman senator | Derek Jacobi |

## Release strategy

Premiered in Los Angeles, *Gladiator* was exhibited on 2,938 screens on its opening weekend in the USA (7 May 2000), with the British opening a week later on 417 screens. The film was released in stages over May and June across the rest of Europe and several other parts of the world. An IMAX version was released in the USA in November 2000.

## Synopsis

Maximus is a brave and respected general in the Roman army fighting in Germany in the first century AD. He is loyal to the Emperor Marcus Aurelius who is killed by his own son, Commodus. Maximus refuses to serve Commodus and is sentenced to death. He escapes but discovers that his family has been brutally murdered on the orders of Commodus. Maximus is taken prisoner by slavers and in North Africa is sold to become a gladiator. Trained by Proximo, a former gladiator, Maximus becomes master of the gladiatorial arena and is sent to Rome to take part in the games being staged by the new Emperor, Commodus. Maximus has vowed vengeance and finds an ally in a former lover, Lucilla, sister of Commodus. Fellow gladiators and certain members of the Roman senate opposed to the increasingly dictatorial rule of Commodus also help Maximus. After various set-backs, he manages to confront Commodus face to face in the Colosseum.

# Introduction

The hero at bay

'So, do you like movies about gladiators?' (Captain Oveur in the 1980 disaster movie spoof *Airplane*)

It would seem that many people do indeed like films featuring gladiators if the success of the 2000 film *Gladiator* is any guide. Yet it could have been a major commercial failure. Its director had not enjoyed recent success at the box office and the film featured no top stars of that time. Its marketing taglines almost seem bloated with hype: 'The general who became a slave ... the slave who became a gladiator ... the gladiator who defied an empire ...' There was a danger that it could be just another mindless blockbuster riddled with cut-out characters and clichés, deservedly dying at the box office.

In fact it was one of the most successful films of its year in financial terms, pleasing large sections of the public, not just hard-core fans, and receiving acclaim from several professional critics. Analysis of its making and reception sheds much light on the workings of the film industry and on audience responses to its products. Part of that appeal is the presence of actors like Russell Crowe who starred as the film's hero, Maximus. Indeed the film could also be said to a good case study of the making of a new major star.

The film is also a fascinating example of how an old film genre that seemingly had passed away could be brought back to life. *Gladiator* stands in a long line of movies which might be grouped under the generic umbrella of 'historical epic'. Though epics have figured prominently in film history, *Gladiator's* director Ridley Scott can be credited with reviving what had long been an ailing genre, especially after the relative failure at the box office of Antony Mann's *Fall of the Roman Empire* in 1964, in the footstep of the previous year's major failure *Cleopatra* (1963).

Subsequent to the success of *Gladiator*, movies in the same vein quickly followed: *Troy* (2004), *King Arthur* (2004) and *Alexander* (2004). In 2004, the ancient British Queen Boadicea, scourge of the Roman invaders, was reported to be the subject of four new movies according to a *Guardian* feature (30 June 2004). Meanwhile, though General Maximus himself may have bit the dust, the *Gladiator* storyline was set to be continued in a sequel, *Gladiator 2*, according to an Internet report posted at http://movies.themovieinsider.com/?mid=992.

The revival of the epic owed much to advances in film-making technology, notably computer-generated imagery. Yet the spectacular effects it can yield are only one of the 'languages' through which a film communicates with its audience. *Gladiator* relies upon carefully chosen images, sounds and text on screen, most of which are delivered by the film camera, microphones and other long-established technologies. Thus, it blends both 'old' and 'new' in communication of plot information about settings, characters, their relationships and the meaning of events on screen as well as the evocation of certain moods at different points in the film.

*Gladiator* was directed by Ridley Scott whose work raises several questions about a major debate in film analysis surrounding 'auteur theory'. The film's story is not complex yet the way in which it is told says much about mainstream narrative techniques. But stories and characters also paint a picture of a wider world, not just that of the film itself. They reflect and address hopes and fears, beliefs and attitudes current in the society at the time of the film's making and reception. Beneath its action–packed scenes and richly detailed sets, *Gladiator* carries specific values and messages which also deserve close scrutiny.

**NOTES:**

# Frameworks for a Film

'What we do in life...' (*Gladiator* tagline)

**No film can be fully understood without looking at the context of its making. The most immediate framework is the film industry itself. Very quickly after their birth in 1895, movies ceased to be the province of amateur enthusiasts.** *Gladiator* **was the product of an industry that had been evolving since the early 1900s, though its shape at the end of the twentieth century was very different to that at its start.**

The following chapter, 'The Movie Industry Today', will explore the main features of the industry today and how it influences what type of movies get made. But no industry exists in isolation. It too is shaped by the cultural, social, legal, economic, technological and environmental contexts in which it exists. *Gladiator* was made during 1999 in a world quite different to that with which, for example, the makers of an earlier epic movie, *Scipione L'Africano* had to function in 1937.

Both are historical epics, but the latter film was a deliberately patriotic spectacle, made to link the glory of ancient Rome to the dictatorial regime of Benito Mussolini which ruled Italy when the movie was made. America in the 1990s was by contrast a 'free' country. Yet the makers of *Gladiator* did not have a free hand to do whatever they liked.

The film industry is part of the overall economy. Its activities will be heavily influenced by its general structure as well as by specific economic factors such as taxation and subsidies. The economic context of *Gladiator* was, in a word, capitalism, in which products are made for the profit of those who own the industries that produce them. In such a system, land, raw material and human skills are commodities to be bought and sold largely according the dictates of profit maximisation.

It is a market-based system in which different sections of the film industry compete against each other, just like car manufacturers or owners of hotel chains. The movie business as a whole has to compete against other industries, especially other media and suppliers of alternative forms of entertainment. The larger firms are corporations, owned by their shareholders, with most shares often owned by investment banks and other big businesses.

Sometimes there are individuals within the company, often the chief executives who are well known to the public and can exercise a strong influence within the company. Steven Spielberg of DreamWorks is one example. Jean-Marie Messier, former Chairman and Chief Executive Officer of Vivendi Universal also played a high profile role, though the word 'former' should serve as a reminder that today's business leaders are not unmovable owners.

Part of the economic context is size and number of firms that own different parts of the film industry. Over the past few decades, a small number of big corporations have come to dominate the film industry. They own not only film production companies but also film distributors. However, their activities are not confined to one sector like film. The two main production companies behind *Gladiator* illustrate several trends.

## Little...

DreamWorks SKG is a comparative newcomer, founded by Steven Spielberg, former Disney film executive Jeffrey Katzenberg and David Geffen whose background was the music business. It produces not only films but also material for TV, DVD, computer games and music. The largest shareholder is actually Microsoft co-founder Paul Allen with a 24% stake of the company. Other shareholders include Starbucks chairman Howard Schultz and former Pepsi chief Roger Enrico.

Capitalism has been described above as a competition-driven market economy. But the economic struggle also encourages the formation of alliances. A description of DreamWorks would not be complete without mention of the alliances it was to form with firms like Burger King, Baskin Robbins and Philips Electronics. Even rival film-makers can form temporary partnerships as with the teaming of DreamWorks and Twentieth Century Fox to produce **Minority Report** (2003). Similarly, Warner Brothers (part of Time Warner) co-financed and distributed Steven Spielberg's *A.I.* (2001).

The various ventures that comprise a business like DreamWorks are themselves commodities, to be bought and sold when deemed commercially appropriate. DreamWorks invested in the GameWorks video arcades with SEGA and Universal Studios but sold its shares in 2001. In 2003, DreamWorks Records was sold to the Universal Music Group. At the same time, UMG parent Vivendi Universal and DreamWorks SKG announced the extension of a film and home video distribution agreement first established in 1995.

## ...and large

Vivendi Universal, the film's co-producer, is actually a better illustration of today's economic framework. Unlike its partner DreamWorks, it is a genuine transnational corporation. The group was formed through a merger between Vivendi, the French telecommunications and water supply giant company, and the American media giant Universal. It also includes one of Europe's largest pay-TV businesses, Canal+.

But capitalism is a dynamic system. Patterns of ownership and production can change rapidly. Furthermore, the dominance of giant media conglomerates like Time Warner, Bertelsmann, News Corporation, Sony and Viacom should not disguise the presence of a myriad of small and medium sized enterprises. Some prosper because of a strong regional base (e.g. certain cinema chains) while others specialise in certain highly technical fields such as special effects (e.g. Industrial Light and Magic or Pixar

**NOTES:**

Animation). There are usually tax advantages too in the formation of a new company for particular projects.

The career of *Gladiator* director Ridley Scott illustrates these points. His first film company was Percy Main Productions (***Thelma and Louise*** (1991), followed by ***1492: Conquest of Paradise*** (1992), both of which he directed). In 1995, along with his brother Tony Scott, he founded Scott Free Productions, a film and television production company (***White Squall*** (1996) followed by ***G.I. Jane*** (1997), which again were both directed by him). In the case of the large budget *Gladiator*, Scott Free teamed up with the much bigger companies DreamWorks and Universal.

The Scott brothers also owned the historic Shepperton Studio (which subsequently merged with neighbouring Pinewood in 2001). Big production companies like MGM, Paramount, Warner Bros., Disney, Universal-owned UK production house Working Title as well as national UK broadcasters have hired its facilities. They also own Mill Film, a state-of-the-art CGI studio in London. Not surprisingly it did many of the special effects for *Gladiator*.

## Global forces

Economies have long ceased to be bound by national borders. Big corporations have production ventures in many countries while selling their products to customers around the globe. In the case of the film industry this trend was well established early in the twentieth century. When the epic ***Ben-Hur*** was screened in 1925, audiences in countries like Britain would be used to watching other American movies at their local cinema. American companies like Paramount also acquired cinemas abroad during the inter-war period.

Yet the British film industry was then and remains now no negligible force. Many films have been made in Britain not just by British film-makers but also by American companies who for financial or technical reasons see advantages to do so. *Gladiator* shows some of the attractions of the UK. One at the time was a system of tax breaks for film-makers. But perhaps a bigger draw is the attraction of a local workforce and production facilities needed to make a film. Some of the older sound stages like Shepperton Studio are especially valued (some of the work on *Gladiator* was done there). British technical staff, from set designers and camera crew to special effects experts, are also well regarded by foreign film-makers.

However, British cinema screens are dominated by American content. At the 2000 box office, *Gladiator* came second, after the (American) ***Toy Story 2*** (1999) (distributed by the American distributors Buena Vista). In the top ten, there was only one film that, by most definitions, would be seen as 'purely' British, ***Billy Elliot*** (2000) in seventh place and even its distribution was handled by the American UIP, the same distributors in Britain of *Gladiator*.

The problems of the British industry are clearly evident. There is a constant difficulty to raise the money in the first place to make a movie, then to find a distributor and get a space on cinema screens dominated, at least at the multiplex, by Hollywood imports. Even the successful ***Billy Elliot*** came nowhere near *Gladiator*'s takings at the British box office (£16,661,492 compared to the latter's £30,907,687).

## International co-productions

There has been a lot of debate about the various economic and cultural phenomena grouped under the term 'globalisation'. In terms of film, one symptom of what, arguably, is an increasingly integrated world is the global movie. Its production company may have branches in several countries or, alternatively, several companies based in different countries might work on it. Money invested in its making might also have such diverse sources while the locations at which it is filmed straddle the globe. The actors, directors and film crew similarly cover many nationalities while the audience at which it is aimed is a global one.

*Gladiator* involved production companies from both sides of the Atlantic: the Hollywood-based DreamWorks and the British Scott Free Productions. It was directed by an Englishman from South Shields now resident in the USA. It starred a New Zealander (resident in Australia). Locations in four different countries were used for the live action *Gladiator*. It was released on a worldwide basis. That said, it is usually the domestic market where most money is made (or, at least, is likely to be made).

Though they are global players, the major film studios still retain a presence in Hollywood (Disney, DreamWorks, MGM/UA) or, alternatively, buy up or merge with companies already based there (e.g. Vivendi/Universal, News Corporation/Twentieth Century Fox, Sony/Columbia). Certainly there are still alternative centres of film-making, notably India. Countries as diverse as the Czech Republic, Iran, China and Brazil have also recently produced critically acclaimed films. Yet the audiences that get to see them are a tiny proportion of those who saw *Gladiator*. Even India's 'Bollywood' movies seem to be losing some of their local distinctiveness.

## US rules?

To some extent, it is fair to talk about Americanisation rather than globalisation. The film production market in the USA was valued at $9.5 billion in 2002, roughly nine times the estimate for France that year. Crucially, American companies have a stranglehold on film distribution. In the case of the UK, the distributors for nine of the top ten box office films for 2000 were all American — Buena Vista, UIP, Columbia Tristar and Twentieth Century Fox. In 2003, Buena Vista and UIP

**NOTES:**

alone distributed 49.1% of all films released in Britain.

Reference has already been made to the dominance of American or American co-produced films on cinema screens around the world. Culturally it acts as a transmission belt for (certain) American values and lifestyles alongside the flood of American sitcoms, soap operas and chat shows onto local television screens. More people are familiar with Disneyfied versions of **Robin Hood** (1973) and **The Jungle Book** (1967) than they are with the originals.

At the same time, local film-makers constantly struggle to survive, though this situation might act as a stimulant to do something different and more creative. Many might favourably compare in terms of inventiveness non-American films like Brazil's **City of God** (2002), Germany's **Run, Lola Run** (1999) or Spain's **All About my Mother** (1999) against the roughly contemporaneous **Gladiator**. It might be noted that cultural influences are not one way: for example, many contemporary American films bear the influence of Hong Kong martial arts cinema.

## Legal constraints

The film industry also operates within the framework of another set of institutions. There is the legal system, both in terms of formal laws on the stature books, government regulations and the precedents set by particular court cases. Legal actions, for example, were one factor that helped to break up the old Hollywood Studio System. Perhaps the key law affecting film-making is that of intellectual property or copyright. Ideas are as jealously guarded as property in land and other physical assets, as was illustrated by the legal suit against DreamWorks and Universal for 'stealing' the idea for the film **Small Soldiers** (1998). **Gladiator** itself was the victim of intensive piracy with illegal DVDs quickly emerging from countries like China.

Laws and regulations constrain film-makers in other ways. They take the form of stringent censorship systems in some countries while, elsewhere, it is a matter of films receiving a classification to indicate their content. However, it must be stressed that the economic imperative to maximise audiences is a far bigger constraint and that the public could be said to constitute the ultimate censors. If **Gladiator** had done badly at the box office, it is doubtful whether the wave of historical epics that followed in its wake would have happened.

The main political context to **Gladiator** is the end of the Cold War, brought about by the collapse of one 'empire' (Communism), and the current supremacy of the remaining superpower, the USA. Many see it too as a kind of empire. Its economy, both as a producer and consumer, dominates the global economic system. Politically, it has taken on the role of (self-appointed) world 'policeman', rooting out opponents wherever they may be lurking.

Yet, it is also an empire externally beset by enemies who seem unwilling to accept defeat. Internally, there is dissension and, in some quarters, much self-doubt. Many of its institutions, including its electoral system, are criticised for corruption while dominant lifestyles are condemned by critics for their self-indulgence and excess (not least in books with titles like *Fat Nation*). New economic competitors, especially in southern and eastern Asia, also threaten its hegemony. Many of these themes are echoed in **Gladiator**.

Economy, technology, law and polity are all then frameworks within which the film industry has to function. Yet all are in turn both influences upon and expressions of a given society, its lifestyles, beliefs and values in a particular historical period.

## Social circles

Modern society is in a state of major flux. There have been huge changes in demography,

settlement patterns and lifestyles. Many media producers of media products, not just films, consciously attune their activities to those changes. For example, the increasing proportion of older people in societies like the UK and USA may well influence film-makers and others to moderate their pursuit of the Holy Grail of the Youth Market, favouring instead products that appeal to those 50 and over. **Gladiator** could be said to have built-in multi-generational appeal.

Women now have a larger voice in most industrial societies. Indeed, the first DreamWorks film, **The Peacemaker** (1997), was directed by a woman, Mimi Leder. Yet most media companies are still dominated by men and that male audiences figure prominently in their perceptions. It is not surprising, then, that male-dominated movies like **Gladiator** continue to flow off the production lines, although it has certain 'feminine' qualities, perhaps mirroring wider changes in contemporary culture.

Taking the population of industrialised countries as a whole, a large percentage now lives in 'edge' developments out in the suburbs. If they do go the cinema, it will be for the most part to the multiplex cinemas that have sprung up on retail parks and other such locations. Not surprisingly, many films will be made that exploit the multiplex screen (and sound system) to full advantage as well as appeal to the kind of audience found there. Certainly it encourages the production of spectacular movies like **Gladiator**. Yet many more people will see the movie on their TV sets, a factor which also informs choices about camera positioning and editing.

Other social and cultural changes are harder to pin down, let alone relate to the production and consumption of movies. Some social critics, for example, claim to have identified something they call the 'sentimentalisation of society'. If true, it would mean that there is a much bigger market for 'corny' stories about

**NOTES:**

heroes and heroic deaths than those of a more cynical disposition might assume.

Last, but not least, modern society is one seemingly gripped by all kinds of doubts, anxieties, fears and phobias. Some seem rather irrational, not least the paranoiac taste for conspiracy theories (tapped by *The X Files*, *The Da Vinci Code*, etc.). Some may be more real such as concerns about community breakdown, economic decline or ecological collapse.

Added together, they create a widespread feeling that 'things aren't what they used to be…', 'the country's going to the dogs…' and that 'politicians are out of touch with ordinary people'. They feed a willingness to look for saviours, perhaps a 'general on a white horse' (many wanted General Colin Powell to stand for President of the USA), a strong man (President Putin of Russia fits that bill) or some outsider, untainted by the corrupt ways of the ruling elite (even Arnold Schwarzenegger!). This is just the right context for a movie about a strong and honest hero saving a civilisation from its own worst excesses.

**NOTES:**

# The Movie Industry Today

'But as for me? I'm an entertainer'
(Proximus in *Gladiator*)

**The credits of *Gladiator* announce that 'Universal Pictures and DreamWorks Pictures present a Douglas Wick production in association with Scott Free'. That acknowledgement spotlights the complex nature of modern film-making but also the many connections with the film industry of the past.**

The most fundamental continuity from the early days of film-making is that most movies are designed to be consumer products. They are not a platform for political advocacy (though certain political values, in the broadest sense, may be present). Nor are they primarily a vehicle for artistic experimentation (though they may feature stylistic innovations). Success is measured in commercial terms.

Furthermore, most films have followed a similar 'life cycle'. Between initial concept and final consumption by a film's audience, this cycle starts with a variety of activities grouped under the heading of 'pre-production', followed by the actual shooting or 'production' of the film, after which comes various kinds of 'post-production' work.

Then follows the 'distribution' stage, which includes the making of copies or 'prints' of the film, actual distribution to the cinemas and, of course, marketing and other forms of publicity that seek to build an audience for the movie. Part of those plans will include choices about when the film will be screened as well as where and in what sequence of locations. Last but not least is the 'exhibition' stage or what Americans call the 'theatrical release' when the film is screened at various cinemas, deals with whose owners will have been struck by the distributors.

One change in recent years is an 'afterlife' following this cycle. In it, a film is transferred to video and DVD for rental and sale, followed by broadcasts on satellite, cable and terrestrial TV. A few films might also be brought back to the cinema, perhaps under the guise of so-called 'manager's choice', when the initial screening plans underestimated its appeal. Alternatively, in the network of regional art house cinemas, it might feature as part of some season such as a retrospective of a director's work. There is always the opposite possibility, namely that the film bypasses the cinema stage altogether, going straight to TV (normally a sign of failure).

The following discussion will focus on the production stages, leaving choices made during the distribution and exhibition stages to the section 'Building an Audience' (pg.19).

## Fixing a deal

Films start life as an idea. It may be an original story or one adapted from another source, be it a straight sequel to an existing movie, a remake of an old movie, a reworking of a foreign language film, an adaptation of a novel, TV programme or some other such text. In between is the grey area of an idea based on real life events, though usually, even in the case of biographical films, the connection is often somewhat tenuous.

Then follow attempts to get backers interested in the funding of the actual movie. Normally financial investors will expect evidence that the chances of a return on their capital are good. It might be that the genre is experiencing a cycle of popularity or that the adaptation is from a book by a best-selling novelist. Further inducement might be provided by proposals to cast certain stars or use a particular successful director.

At this stage, a deal is coming together. Unlike the days of the old Hollywood studio system, where films rolled continuously off the studio production lines and where stars, directors and crew were told what to do, complex negotiations will be necessary before the final 'package' emerges. It is most likely to be a 'one-off' production, with new negotiations necessary if it is decided to produce a follow-up sequel or prequel.

The modern studio itself has become more a distributor than a film-maker per se. It may make some movies but the major ones like Disney, Warners and Universal are more likely to invest monies in separate production companies. Some of these such as Fox Searchlight, New Line Cinema and Touchstone Pictures are actually subsidiaries of the major media corporations. Disney's Miramax sometimes produces movies with potentially controversial content that might otherwise undermine the 'wholesome family entertainment' brand of its parent.

Other studios are fully independent. Thus 'Dog Eat Dog' is the film production company owned by Michael Moore, Tribeca belongs in part to actor Robert de Niro, while Haxan Films is the home of the team that produced *The Blair Witch Project* (1999). Sometimes, smaller companies have production and financing deals with the big studios as in the case of Woody Allen's Gravier Productions with DreamWorks or Clint Eastwood's Malpaso with Warners. Thus, many 'independents' are quite dependent in reality.

## A new studio?

DreamWorks, formed in 1994, falls somewhere between the major transnational conglomerates and the small-scale independent studios. It is sufficiently large to be able to attract venture capital for its film projects, though its attractions owe much to the presence of Steven Spielberg in its management. The company is not confined to film, having been active across several media: TV programme making, the production of video and DVD, computer games and, for a while, music records.

It has no cinema 'wing', unlike the old Hollywood studios such as Paramount whose films had their first run in Paramount-owned cinemas before being sold to other cinema chains. Even more crucially, being a

**NOTES:**

comparative newcomer, it has no extensive back catalogue of movies. In the case of old companies, this constitutes a veritable treasure hoard of 'content' to fill cable and satellite channel airtime as well as new DVDs, which is why, of course, corporations like Sony want to gain control of companies like MGM. In spring 2003, DreamWorks had some 45 films in its library compared to Universal's 1500, according to *Business Week* (23 May 2003).

DreamWorks does have a distribution network in the USA but not abroad which makes it dependent on the deal it made with Universal and United International Pictures (UIP). Such relationships mean that some of the profit has to be shared which was a major reason why the old Hollywood studios tried to keep production, distribution and exhibition under one business umbrella. According to the same *Business Week* report, in 2003 DreamWorks was paying Universal $60 million a year to use its distribution network outside the USA.

The leading personnel reflect the way DreamWorks tried to construct a base that went beyond pure film-making. Spielberg had enjoyed great critical and commercial success in live movies. Jeffrey Katzenberg was experienced in film-making, especially animation, and TV. David Geffen, on the other hand, provided music business expertise. Walter Parkes and Laurie McDonald were brought from Amblin (Spielberg's own production company) to oversee live action films (of which *Gladiator* was to be one).

Launched as a private company, DreamWorks was freed from the constant pressure to yield dividend for the shareholders to whom business quoted on the Stock Exchange are beholden. To some extent, this gave extra creative freedom. Of course, it too needs money, much of it coming from a credit facility negotiated with the Chemical Banking Corporation. Paul Allen, Microsoft's co-founder, took a 21% share in DreamWorks for the princely sum of $500 million.

DreamWorks produces a fairly limited number of films, whether under its auspices or 'outsourced' to other production companies. Old-style studios like Paramount were able to keep a much bigger output of movies (at its height, an average of one a week). There were certain advantages. There was more chance that there would a big box office hit among those releases, one whose earnings might well offset disappointing returns elsewhere. The continuity in employment under the contract system also allowed workers, from directors downwards, to hone their skills. And last, the same sets, props and costumes, could be recycled, with a few alterations, into new movies, with correspondingly lowered production costs.

DreamWorks has no such advantages and this is why, when added to the competitiveness of the modern entertainment market, its business position is comparatively insecure, no matter how illustrious some of its leading figures. One consequence is a need to find partners to co-finance deals. *Gladiator* illustrates this practice with the names of not just DreamWorks but also Universal stamped on the film This also explain why so much was spent on advertising the film ($42,700,000, though this figure includes the cost of prints). It is simply a way of reducing the risk of box office failure.

## Money matters

Some finance for a film may come from the film studio in its capacity as a distributor. Other sources include loans from banks and other financial institutions, equity investors (who thereby get a claim on part of the future profits), monies from pre-sales to cable networks and other such outlets as well as merchandising and product placement deals. In countries like Britain, television companies like the BBC and Channel 4 have also put significant investment into film-making. The complexities of these deals are sometimes reflected in the rather long list of companies named in the film credits.

But a success 'output' often (though not always) depends on expensive inputs, not least 'awesome' special effects, and saturation marketing, including simultaneous opening across the country at the same weekend. This in turn necessitates more costly prints (roughly £1,000 a copy). These are all extra costs which, in turn, will have to be covered by extra earnings if the film is going to deliver a profit.

Film audiences and therefore box office takings have been recovering in recent years. However, the average cost of making movies and especially 'blockbusters' has been rising faster and the cost of marketing those movies has risen faster still. The *average* cost of a mainstream film rose tenfold from 1971 ($7.5 million, adjusted for inflation) to 1997 ($75.5 million).

Competition for cinema screens itself has increased with the major studios releasing not only more films but also seeking to 'four-wall' them (i.e. arrange a wide release north, south, east and west). Greater spending on advertising in turn encourages a wide release strategy in order to justify the marketing plan. All this is happening when the rival attractions of TV channels also keep growing in number and diversity while home entertainment systems on which they can be watched become more impressive.

The dangers are obvious. According to Frank Mancuso, a veteran Hollywood executive, *'we've lost our sense of restraint, continually overproducing and overbuilding'* (quoted in *Sight and Sound* Mediawatch 2001). The industry is still haunted by the devastating blow administered to United Artists by the box office failure of the 1980 epic western *Heaven's Gate*. One consequence was an increased wariness about backing would-be 'auteurs' whose heavily personal way of making movies might also mean dangerous cost overruns.

It might not seem sensible to spend so much money on comparatively few films. Yet the

**NOTES:**

enormous profits made by films like *Titanic* (1997) are tantalising. *Gladiator*'s release was a success. Yet, pleasing though that might be to its makers, it also had the effect of eating into the market for movies released at the same time, perhaps to the overall detriment of the film industry. It also reduces the diversity in the films available for audiences since there is such a strong incentive to 'play safe'.

## Market pitch

It has become a commonplace to describe many multiplex blockbuster movies as 'high concept' movies. Far from being some high-minded intellectually complex and artistically rich film, such a movie is a carefully tailored product aimed at maximising the return on the monies invested in its making. Such films are deliberately engineered to be big draws and crowd pleasers.

The financial imperatives described above are the driving force. Another factor was the surprise success of *Jaws* in the summer of 1975 and the perception that it was possible to devise a formula to repeat its triumph at the box office. The need to sell films to TV networks as well as create made-for-TV-movies that could easily be advertised on the networks before actual broadcast gave added impetus to the search for a template for success. Intensified advertising also encouraged film producers to think in terms of movies with built-in marketing angles, including sequences tailor-made for trailer clips as well as spin-off products.

In practice there is no foolproof recipe for success. If there were, every film would be a box office triumph. George Lucas might seem to have found one with the *Star Wars* (1977) 'franchise'. Yet his *Willow* (1986) was a comparative failure.

None the less, mainstream movie business feels that a number of ingredients give greater chance of success in the mass market. The result is the high concept formula, examples of

which include *Ghostbusters* (1984), *Top Gun* (1986), *Batman* (1989), *Under Siege* (1992), *Speed* (1994), *Twister* (1996), *Con Air* (1997), *Armageddon* (1998), *Pearl Harbor* (2001) and *The Last Samurai* (2004). Producers Don Simpson and Jerry Bruckheimer were behind many high concept films, though Barry Diller and Michael Eisner are often credited with creating the term when they were young executives at ABC TV.

Ideally, the combination of such ingredients leads to the release of the movie becoming an 'event'. This means that, with the aid of careful marketing and good publicity, it has turned into a 'must-see' movie, one whose arrival millions keenly await. Thus it might make an otherwise dull weekend or holiday season into a memorable break.

## High concept *Gladiator*?

*Gladiator* conforms to the formula in some ways but not others:

**A single strong idea which can be easily pitched to potential backers as well as translated seamlessly into a marketing strategy.** The storyline is likely to be one that can be summed up in a few words while the title of the film might similarly give an instant idea of what the film is about. It is not hard to guess what *Gladiator* would be about and its story could be summed up in a less than 25 words.

**Distinctiveness in the sense that the film will somehow stand out from its rivals, even if, in other ways, it might be quite hackneyed.** *Gladiator*'s setting in ancient Rome would be a novelty for those used only to films set in the here and now or in the future.

**A strong element of universality.** The film's characters and situations could be understood across many countries and cultures. Maximus may be an extraordinary man yet his character and motives are easy to grasp.

**A simple plot.** *Gladiator* is a straightforward tale of revenge, with few complications. The narrative progresses as the hero overcomes one obstacle after another on his mission.

**Adrenaline-fuelled action thrillers though with other genre conventions mixed in.** There is plenty of action but *Gladiator* is not a hybrid movie but a straightforward historical epic.

**Stars often play the same role based on original success** (sometimes TV, not necessarily film). Stars are often chosen to appeal to specific audience segments, which when added together, create one big audience. Here, *Gladiator* breaks with the formula. Russell Crowe cannot be compared to the likes of Tom Cruise or Will Smith.

**'One note' minor characters.** Their attitudes and behaviour can be easily grasped while the actors who play them are often chosen for their looks which lend themselves to easy stereotyping. Here *Gladiator* mainly follows the template. There is even a gentle giant who dies a noble death (Hagen).

**A simple narrative structure.** *Gladiator* certainly starts with a 'hot' first act, with subsequent crises and worsening danger coming to a dramatic climax, plus salvation (albeit in different ways) for the major characters. True to the template a 'feel-good' ending is engineered.

**A film style with heavy use of montages.** This description might apply to the opening battle scene and some gladiator fights. Indeed several parts of the film could be easily translated into posters, trailers and publicity stills. But at other times, there are extended sequences of dialogue where little action happens.

**A glossy graphic sheen.** The film is certainly very polished but does not quite have the glossy sheen of *Titanic* nor the computer game

**NOTES:**

qualities of the *Matrix* films (1999, 2003). Set well in the past, it necessarily lacks the ultra-high technology and super-industrial design of *The Terminator* (1984).

**Heavy use of music, often rock or dance, that often bears little or no relation to the actual narrative.** Here *Gladiator* parts company with the likes of *Top Gun* and *Titanic*.

**Frequent allusions to other films as well as TV programmes.** There are only very minor instances of this, e.g. Maximus' horses are called, in translation, 'Trigger' (horse of the singing cowboy Roy Rogers), and 'Silver' (as in the *Lone Ranger*).

**Over-the-top macho action** (by women as well as men). It is certainly very violent in parts but only as demanded by the narrative, unlike *Die Hard* (1988) and *Lethal Weapon* (1987).

**'Awesome' special effects and other breath-taking moments in the story.** Here *Gladiator* certainly matches the template.

**Much use of irony and detached not-taking-this-too-seriously tone.** It lacks such ironical 'tie-in-cheek' qualities of many of the films noted before. Indeed, Maximus exhibits an unusual tendency towards despondency and even despair (most high concept heroes just make casual asides while drawing their breath).

**A constant eye to merchandising possibilities.** *Gladiator* cannot be compared to movies that have created a mountain of toys, T-shirts and the like.

*Gladiator*, then, was in many ways an 'old-fashioned' film. It certainly includes some of the high concept ingredients but not all. Perhaps the most striking difference is in its social setting. Many high concept movies are based around 'ordinary guys' (and the odd girl) caught in extraordinary situations as in *Speed* (1994). *Gladiator*, by contrast, is quite patrician. It seldom strays outside the ranks of the high and mighty. Its hero is a Roman general, his enemy the new Emperor. Maximus does encounter 'ordinary' gladiators but he is soon back among Rome's elite, mixing with senators like Gracchus and the Emperor's sister, Lucilla. Common Roman citizens are little more than a crowd, just as in the older generation of epics.

## A crisis of creativity?

According to the *Gladiator*'s executive producer Walter Parkes, *'in the last 15 to 20 years of movies, many of the most successful ones have been about rediscovery of classic genres either through modern writing or even more importantly digital technology.'* If franchise films (*Scream* (1996), etc.) as well as genuine prequels and sequels were added to Parke's list, there is an unavoidable feeling of an industry whose creative juices are getting rather low.

Certainly there may well be economic savings to be made in repetition and the reworking of existing raw material, rather than risky innovation. In purely creative terms, it is easier to adapt what exists than generate new ideas. *Gladiator* could be said to be a 'retro' film. It looks back to the old Italian 'monumental' films of the period just before World War I (e.g. *Cabiria* (1914) and *Quo Vadis* (1951)), early Hollywood epics (*Intolerance* (1916) and the first *Ben-Hur*, etc.), the sword-wielding 'swashbuckler' heroes (e.g. *Adventures of Robin Hood* (1938)), and the cinemascope spectacles of the 50s (*The Robe* (1953), *El Cid* (1961) and, of course, the second *Ben-Hur* (1959)).

*Gladiator* is old-fashioned in other ways. No major 'love interest' was included, unlike comparable films such as *Braveheart* (1995) (the bizarre romance of William Wallace and the French princess). Little attempt was made to 'beef up' the female parts, unlike the film adaptation of *Lord of the Rings* (2001-3). It also resisted any employment of Hong Kong martial arts movie elements. For example,

*Brotherhood of the Wolf* (2002), a film set in eighteenth century France, was in part a 'retro' film paying tribute to the 1930s Universal monster movies. But it came complete with characters jumping and kicking in the best John Woo fashion… not so *Gladiator*.

## New ingredients

In terms of film style, *Saving Private Ryan* (1998) had set new benchmarks for the depiction of combat. They had been consolidated in the TV series *Band of Brothers* (2001). It would seem almost natural to graft such a look onto the narrative elements of those older action films. As Parkes suggests, new techniques in fields such as computer graphics could make the resultant film feel new as well as look spectacular. The more 'modern' characterisation of Maximus, discussed later, combined with the comparatively youthful but still 'manly' appearance of actor Russell Crowe could also prevent the film from feeling too old.

The film also bolts on bits and pieces from contemporary psychotherapy and 'confessional culture'. Commodus might seem a prime candidate for Oprah Winfrey, given the way he whinges about his personal 'issues'. *Gladiator* is tough on badness but attempts to understand the causes of badness. Most 'bad guys' of 50s and 60s epics were just plain … bad.

That said, *Gladiator* still reflects a certain creative stagnation on the part of most 'mainstream' film-making at present. This is not to deny its entertainment value. After all, many people watch their favourite films and TV shows over and over again. Familiarity breeds pleasure, not just contempt. But there is arguably more energy and imagination evident in comparatively inexpensive films like *Good-bye Lenin!* (Germany, 2003) or *City of God* (Brazil, 2002) or the more 'leftfield' movies emanating from the USA such as *Being John Malkovich* (1999) than in *Gladiator* and fellow mainstream products.

**NOTES:**

# Film Genre and *Gladiator*

'My name is gladiator' (Maximus in *Gladiator*)

**A film text exists in a variety of contexts. One is the body of films that have preceded it. Both the decisions of film-makers and the expectations and responses of their audiences are influenced by the way certain ingredients seem to be repeated from one film to another, forming discrete categories of film. There are many variations within these 'genres' but their general outlines persist.**

Genres draw upon a fundamental human need to describe and classify. Such 'typologies' help us to conduct activities, not least to anticipate, understand and make sense of things. Life would be rather short if we did not distinguish the edible from the inedible or the poisonous from what is safe. Most sports would be unplayable if the participants did not jointly agree the rules of the game.

Across the arts too, both creators and consumers have thought in generic terms, from plays (e.g. comedies versus tragedies) to paintings ('impressionist', 'cubist', 'still life', etc.). Music is similarly perceived in terms of form or content ('symphony', 'quartet', 'reggae', 'blues', etc.). Film is no exception.

Few creative people in the film industry such as scriptwriters and directors will come to a new movie with absolutely blank minds. Consciously or otherwise, they will be inspired in their efforts by the existing body of films and the patterns created by specific film genres: typical stories, narrative structures, settings, props, costumes, lighting, camerawork, presence of certain stars and certain physical forms (typical shape, length, etc.), to name but a few.

To use a cookery metaphor, genres might be seen as jars of ingredients that can be cooked in different ways. Chefs do not need to rigidly follow set recipes but none the less they conjure up a meal with certain possibilities

already in their heads. Similarly film creatives might stick closely to a formula (as in the Bond movies), take advantage of the opportunity to add or subtract ingredients, or pick and mix from other genres. By doing so, they may push an exiting genre in new directions, perhaps creating whole new sub-genres within it. Alternatively, they may create multi-genre or 'hybrid' films.

Genres may be categorised in many different ways. It may be by medium (e.g. 'film genre') or by form (film ratio/widescreen, running time, colour/black-and-white, live/animated, etc.). It could be done on the basis of purpose (e.g. to shock, to thrill, to make laugh, to persuade, to document, etc.) or the nature of its content (factual documentaries, fictional stories or, again, combinations thereof as in spoof documentaries).

Another possible basis is actual content, its organisation (old film serials or sequence of plot points), narrative structures and devices (e.g. typical characters and situations) or broader themes and ideologies (e.g. crime doesn't pay, dangers of new technology, importance of loyalty). Genres might be distinguished by the way such content is treated or by style (e.g. typical settings, sets, props, lighting, camera technique, editing style). The same content could communicate quite different things by alterations to such stylistic devices. Last but not least they may be distinguished by their link, if any, to 'reality' and to the degree of 'realism' to which they aspire.

It cannot be stressed too strongly that such typical elements or 'conventions' are not fixed rules. They are not like the strict procedures a car plant may follow in the manufacture of vehicles (though even there one might distinguish the 'genre' of family saloons from minis and sports cars).

Film genre conventions, by contrast, permit creative usage by directors and other creative

artists, unlike what might be called formula films which seldom vary. None the less, most films can be understood in relation to one or more established genres. That said, some films defy any such genre analysis, so distinctive is their style or content. In such cases, an understanding of the director, the studio, the country or historical period in which it was made might shed more light on its origins and nature.

## Genre, industry and audience

Genres serve a somewhat different purpose for film producers, distributors, exhibitors and retailers. Indeed the evolution of discrete genres has resulted mainly from their desire to repeat what seemed to appeal to audiences. If film-goers liked films featuring a sheriff and his posse chasing outlaws, then understanding film companies were quick to make more of the same but with sufficient differences so that audiences could be enticed back into the cinema.

With regard to film audiences in particular, genres offer the dual pleasures of familiarity and surprise. In a media-saturated society, even those who do not like movies will find it hard to remain totally unaware of westerns, sci-fi films, horror movies, musicals and the like. Most cinema-goers will have some expectations of what they are about to see before a film starts. Some of that information may have come from the film's marketing but their general expectations will be influenced by that whole body of films they have seen before as well as ones they have read or heard about. This sets up even more possibilities from the film-maker's perspective since they can satisfy those expectations or manipulate them to creative effect.

It might be argued that film-makers are free to invent what they like, within the confines of budgets and available technology. Of course, individuals are equally free to put on whatever clothes they like. Yet certain things do seem to somehow go together while onlookers are going

**NOTES:**

to make certain deductions from what individuals wear, irrespective of actual intentions.

Similarly much of the understanding of and responses to a film by its audiences will be based on comparisons they make between its characters, situations, themes and other ingredients and those in films from the same genre. They might not actually use words like 'genre' but they still think largely within that framework. Video rental stores are well aware of that so they often group films by genre on the shelves (just as many bookshops have separate sections for crime and other genres of fiction).

Film genres have not emerged solely from the hands of studios and directors. Most have roots outside the industry. One such root is reality itself. There was a real 'Wild West' before 'Westerns'. But other cultural forms also played a part. Thus 'Wild West' shows (Buffalo Bill, etc.) and dime novels created many elements that were to be taken up by Hollywood (with as much relation to historical reality). 'Gothic' horror novels sowed the seeds of horror films but there is also real life horror in the form of actual plagues and psychopaths.

Movie genres also evolve due to other forces beyond film-makers. Thus science fiction has shifted from positive visions of new technological advances to much more pessimistic fears about future dystopias largely as a result of a general disenchantment with science and technology across society in the wake of Hiroshima and other horrors. In the aftermath of the 11 September 2001 attacks on the USA, it is likely that the general public may have less taste for comic book stories of evil terrorists in the manner of the *Die Hard* films. By contrast, fears about coming ecological disasters may revive the market for apocalyptic disasters movies like *The Day After Tomorrow* (2004).

Very crudely, film genres can be divided into two broad families. One is melodrama, with its focus on personal emotions and relationships. The other is action, with an emphasis on thrills and spills. Of course, many a war movie may have a scene where soldiers sit quietly thinking about home, perhaps looking at a photograph of loved ones. Thus both *Zulu* (1964, the tale of the battle of Rorke's Drift) and *Saving Private Ryan* (Normandy campaign) feature quiet passages where soldiers wonder about the meaning of the suffering around them and reminisce about home and loved ones, often prior to renewed combat. Indeed in both, such scenes occur just before the final climactic bout of blood-letting.

Within that broad umbrella of the action film, there are many genres and sub-genres. Thus some crime thrillers focus more on the police, others on criminals. Then there are those (e.g. 'heist' movies) that concentrate on the crime itself and how it is going to be perpetrated (or how it went wrong and who was to blame). Police movies can come in the form of films that look carefully at the actual procedures of investigations and ones that feature a 'lone cop', struggling not only against crime but the deadweight of police bureaucracy.

Study of film genre is, then, really about possible ingredients and the way specific movies may use them.

## Epic

*Gladiator* generally follows the conventions of one such genre, the historical epic. The word 'epic' is, however, a rather slippery term. Certainly it sheds light on films clearly related to *Gladiator* like *The Fall of the Roman Empire*, *El Cid* and *Ben-Hur*. Yet other films from self-evidently different genres might also be described as 'epics'.

Some biographical movies or 'biopics' might be described in such a way, not least *Gandhi* (1982) and *Lawrence of Arabia* (1962). Many war movies like *Waterloo* (1970), *The Longest Day* (1962), *A Bridge Too Far* (1977), *Gettysburg* (1993) and *Saving Private Ryan*

deliver large-scale spectacle as do films from other genres. For example, John Ford's *The Searchers* (1956), one of the truly great Westerns, has epic proportions, its tale of a vengeful search stretching over the years. More recently, *Dances With Wolves* (1990) told a tale of similarly large-scale dimensions.

Melodramas, with their focus on individual relationships do tend to be much smaller scale and more intimate but not always. *Gone With The Wind* (1939) features spectacular action and enormous crowd scenes along with larger-than-life characters as did film adaptations of novels like *War and Peace* (1956) and *Doctor Zhivago* (1965). So the term 'epic' is not a precise one.

It might also be noted that other film genres share certain features with the epics noted above. This is most obviously the case with the so-called 'disaster movie'. Its hallmark scenes of devastation on a colossal scale (the sinking of *Titanic* in the eponymous movie or the obliteration of America's eastern seaboard in *The Day After Tomorrow*, for example) mirror those in films like *Intolerance* (1916), especially the latter's spectacular picture of the destruction of Babylon.

The storyline of *Gladiator* shares larger-than-life treachery and betrayal with many other epics yet, it might be noted, many a hero in 'westerns' has saddled up in vengeful pursuit of wrong-doers. Sport movies often feature a narrative in which some team of perennial losers or congenital misfits, manages to overcome seemingly superior opponents – *Cool Runnings* (1993), *Bad News Bears* (1976), *Dodgeball* (2004), etc. – just like the initially disparate band of Proximo's gladiators initially are the underdogs.

## A tale of two gladiators

Even within the more specific realm of films set in ancient Rome featuring gladiators, it is clear that the notion of an epic film genre should not be understood in fixed ways. Many

**NOTES:**

commentators on *Gladiator* understandably drew parallels with Stanley Kubrick's *Spartacus* (1960).

There are certainly many similarities. *Spartacus* is also a story about gladiators fighting back against those who have done them wrong. It features a figure of heroic stature just like Maximus, who also dies gallantly at the end of the film. Part of the story is set in a school of gladiators whose manager Batiatus is not unlike Promixo in *Gladiator*. There are also treacherous politicians, notably Crassus who bears a certain similarity to *Gladiator*'s Commodus. At certain points in both films, masks and disguises figure prominently. Both movies deliver battle scenes with much hand-to-hand fighting both on the battlefield and in the gladiatorial arena.

Yet, there are striking differences. Kubrick's movie is more evidently 'artistic'. The characters, notably Crassus, are much more complex. The narrative also features intricate subtexts of bisexual relations (scenes censored in the first theatrical release) compared to which *Gladiator* is somewhat conventional (though there are hints that the attitude of Commodus towards his sister is not altogether straightforward). Above all, there are richer political themes with issues of oppression, social struggle and freedom being explored more explicitly and in greater depth.

Yet the concept of genre remains a valid one. It may be best understood in terms of distinctive ingredients on which film-makers draw and which in turn guide audiences of what they expect to see on the screen as well as shape their understanding of and responses to what they are seeing. *Gladiator* and *Spartacus* are made using the same set of raw material but the end product is not the same, just as different meals will be cooked by different chefs using similar recipes.

One further proof of a genre's identity is the making of films that spoof it. Thus the Monty Python team produced their satire of the epic, *The Life of Brian* (1979) as did Mel Brooks in *History of the World: Part I* (1981). The Asterix series of cartoons might be included here. None would have been possible if there were not some original to spoof.

## Variations on a theme

The historical epic genre might be broken into several sub-genres though all share the same general characteristics: their characters (real or fictitious) come clothed in sumptuous costumes, playing out the stories against a backdrop of monumental sets, populated by the proverbial 'cast of thousands'. There is the pure sword-and-sandals variant firmly rooted in Grecco-Roman times (including legends from that period): examples include *The Sign of the Cross* (1932), *The Last Days of Pompeii* (1935), *Demetrius and the Gladiators* (1954), *The Sign of the Pagan* (1954), *Alexander the Great* (1956), *Spartacus*, *The 300 Spartans* (1962) and *The Fall of the Roman Empire*.

Ancient Egypt has largely been the setting for horror films (*The Mummy* (1990), etc.), but epics were set there also, e.g. *The Egyptian* (1954). Recognisably similar are movies set in medieval times but replete with similar stories and spectacle such as *The Crusades* (1935), *The Adventures of Robin Hood, Ivanhoe* (1952), *Knights of the Round Table* (1953), *The Adventures of Quentin Durward* (1959), *El Cid, Excalibur* (1981) and *Braveheart*.

Christ and Christianity constitute another discrete sub-genre: *Judith of Bethulia* (1914), *Samson and Delilah* (1949), *Salome* (1953), *The Robe* (1953), *David and Bathsheba* (1951), *Solomon and Sheba* (1959) *King of Kings* (1961), *Barabbas* (1962), *The Greatest Story Ever Told* (1965) and *The Bible* (1966). As in their epic cousins, spectacular special effects abound, be it the parting of the Red Sea in *The Ten Commandments* (1956) or the destruction of entire cities as in *Sodom and Gomorrah* (1962).

Then there is the film that actually takes elements from two sub-genres, notably *Intolerance* and *Ben-Hur*. The latter deals with the story of Christ and the crucifixion. But it is perhaps most well known because of the sea battle and especially spectacular chariot race between the two protagonists, the eponymous hero and yet another treacherous Roman leader, the Tribune Messala, against whom Ben-Hur has vowed vengeance.

The sword-and-sandals epic 'family tree' contains some noble members, none more so than *Spartacus*. But there are also branches with less worthy qualities. Many emanated from Italy ('Hollywood-on-Tiber', though much shooting was done in eastern Europe), with taglines like 'The stupendous saga of the mightiest of mortals' (*Provenzano*, 2000). Perhaps anticipating Ridley Scott's project, some of these films had names like *Invincible Gladiator* (1962), *Rebel Gladiator* (1962) and *Gladiators Seven* (1962). Perhaps their main offspring was Arnold Schwarzenegger (*Conan the Barbarian* (1982), etc.). The 1974 film *The Arena* with nude female gladiators (it was also released under the name *Naked Warriors*) demonstrates how sand-and-sandals films could be turned into crude exploitation movies.

The epic could be 'hybridised' with other genres, while retaining its core characteristics. Thus there is a dose of horror (including Christopher Lee) in *Hercules in the Captive World* (1961). A TV series *Xenia: Warrior Princess* (1995) mixed in elements from Fable and Fantasy. *Hercules Against the Moon Men* (1965) and *Giant of Metropolis* (1963) might even be said to make nods towards sci-fi, the latter featuring a giant ray. The addition of comic book elements produced *The Incredible Hulk* (1978, TV). Politically some were quite radical. In contrast to *Gladiator, Coriolanus* (1964) depicts the Roman Senate as the oppressor of the people.

The boundaries of the Epic, like any other film

**NOTES:**

genre, are fluid. The notion of an Imperial Realm turned rotten is a common ingredient of many epics, not least **Gladiator**. But evil empires occur elsewhere, most notably in fable-and-fantasy films ('sword-and-sorcery' is an alternative name). The most well-known example is probably **Star Wars** with its decadent emperor, evil advisor and their space warrior opponents. **Flash Gordon** similarly had to combat the imperial ambitions of Ming the Merciless in the 1930s comics and movie versions.

Nor is martyrdom in the manner of Maximus confined to epics. Combat film heroes such as Sergeant Stryker (**Sands of Iwo Jima** (1949)) and Captain Miller (**Saving Private Ryan**) pay the ultimate price in their rendezvous with destiny. It is not any specific ingredient but rather the overall combination that gives a genre its identity.

## Up, down and up again

Many epics feature a narrative based on the structure in which the main character falls from power but manages to resurrect his fortunes (there are far more epic heroes than heroines). The epic genre has itself suffered similar fortunes. Following the disappointing performance of **Cleopatra** and **Fall of the Roman Empire** in the 1960s, the following decades saw few historical epics in the traditional sense and no sword-and-sandals movie until **Gladiator**.

Various dynamics would appear to be at work. Audience tastes may simply change. What was once stunningly larger-than-life is then perceived as tiresomely overblown. Ironically the very larger-than-life qualities that helped epics to compete against the pull of the (small) TV screen also served to alienate audiences who came to see the genre as self-indulgently grandiose, with plot and character development lost in a welter of lavish sets, muscle-bound heroes, and predictable setpieces.

But audience tastes can change again and a

door might be opened for the revival of a moribund genre. Perhaps a particularly creative director might breathe fresh life into it (e.g. John Carpenter and horror films or Martin Scorsese and gangster movies). As is argued below, popular interest in the Grecco-Roman period had not disappeared.

Changing technology also plays a major part in encouraging film makers to revisit old genres. New special effects techniques helped with sci-fi ('realistic' aliens thanks both to advances in prosthetics and, later, CGI). The epic film revival certainly owed much to this factor, though it is easy to exaggerate the importance of CGI.

While the history of the genre itself has been something of a rollercoaster, some specific stories and characters have done the cinema 'rounds' more than once, sometimes from the hands of the same film-makers. **Ben-Hur**, for example, first saw life courtesy of director Fred Niblo under the name **Ben-Hur: A Tale of the Christ** (1926). Cecil DeMille recycled his own silent film **The Ten Commandments** (1923) as a technicolour blockbuster three decades later in 1956. Indeed several epics have been re-made, including **Quo Vadis?** (1913, remade 1951) and **King of Kings** (1927, remade 1961).

**Gladiator** draws directly on the Anthony Mann film **The Fall of the Roman Empire**. But that is not the only direct antecedent. Combat against tigers was a feature of the 1954 cinemascope film **Demetrius and the Gladiators**. **Barabbas** also featured gladiator training, animals, trap doors, scenery, elaborate 'plays', including boat battles on artificial oceans. The (slight) religious elements of the film (as raised in dialogue between Juba and Maximus) were fairly commonplace in the older generation of movies, for example, the later **Ben-Hur** and **Barabbas**. The townscapes of the village where Proximus has his school owe much to films like the biblical epic **Sodom and Gomorrah**.

## Reviving a genre

Though the epic film might have gone into a decline in the cinema, public interest in the terrain covered in the movies had itself not waned. Indeed popular enthusiasm for history has if anything strengthened, a phenomenon both reflected in and encouraged by television. 'Pop' history, archaeology programmes (*Time Team*, etc.), dramas (*I Claudius*, etc.) and 'reality TV' shows where contestants have to live as in ancient or medieval times have flowered in recent years. Even situation comedies have put their foot in Roman waters (*Up Pompeii*).

A number of book clubs cater for the same tastes with lavish coffee table tomes about the glories of Roman and other ancient civilisations. Some crime writers, notably Lindsay Davies, have struck gold by setting their mysteries in such worlds. Historical remains like Hadrian's Wall, various surviving Roman viaducts and of course, sites in cities like Rome and Athens all attract huge numbers of tourists.

Given such evidence of public interest, it seems reasonable to assume that the film industry might be persuaded that it could be worth dusting down the historical epic movie and seeing if there is still an audience out there. Such temptation would also be increased by the success of visually stunning blockbusters such as **Independence Day** (1996) and **Titanic**, spectacles that the historical epics might rival.

A successful Shakespeare adaptation set in ancient Rome, Julie Taymor's **Titus** (1999) directly anticipated **Gladiator**. It too had a plot based on revenge while the carnage that ensued yielded little in gore to Ridley Scott's tale of conflict. Like the publicity for **Gladiator**, the big quad posters advertising **Titus** similarly harnessed public interest in ancient Rome by featuring the main characters against the background of the Roman Colosseum.

**NOTES:**

# Film Genre and *Gladiator*

## Risky business

*Gladiator*'s epic character needs little explication: it is set well in the historical past (second century AD). It features a huge cast of extras, spectacular events, larger-than-life characters and a grand storyline. Like the medieval **El Cid** or the biblical **Ben-Hur**, the narrative is structured around the fall of the hero from his high position in society and his subsequent struggles, leading to a climax where he confronts the architect of his misfortunes.

Yet there were differences. King (2002) notes a significant shift in how the sense of spectacle is generated. He shows that there are far fewer long shots, with wide panoramic views in the film compared to **Spartacus**. Correspondingly there are far more close-ups (roughly 50% of the film, over three times the percentage of **Spartacus**). Another interesting contrast might be with the **Fall of the Roman Empire** which lovingly dwells on the large setpiece scenes in Rome where Scott quickly cuts to close-ups of Commodus and his exchanges with Gracchus and the senators.

King rightly emphasises that it is rapid editing and violently unsteady camerawork with which we the viewers are plunged into the mêlée (in the opening battle and gladiatorial contests) that generate the 'in-the-face' spectacle. Several factors might explain why **Gladiator** makes such departures. One is the need to shoot a film in a way that it will still look good on television (where the film will ultimately find its largest audience). Second is the influence of films like **Saving Private Ryan**.

Then there is the need to balance action scenes (assumed to be of greater appeal to young men) with ones devoted to character development and personal relationships, which it may be assumed may be of greater appeal to women (Lads' magazines like *Loaded* or *Nuts* as well as equivalent male–oriented TV shows are not noted for their sensitivity). These are sweeping generalisations. None the less an industry like movie-making has to make broad assumptions about groups of likely consumers since it can scarcely personalise its products.

It has been widely observed, of course, that the increasingly complex cultural patterns in society after World War II, coupled to the growth of rival attractions to cinema, have made it hard for the film industry to predict what movies will be a success. Certainly, it was easier to be fairly certain about attracting an audience in the days when cinema-going was almost a routine social ritual on a mass scale (the peak came in 1946).

In recent decades, such assurance has almost disappeared. Today, the expenditure of many, many million dollars on the story of a Roman general can only constitute a major risk. Films that might have been reasonably assumed to be a fair certainty for success (**Godzilla** (1998) being a good example) failed to take off at the box office. That said, the financial returns on the monies invested in a film **Gladiator** might also be quite monumental as well.

**NOTES:**

Yet more danger for the hero ©*Joel Finler Archive*

**'Conjure magic for them'** (Gracchus in *Gladiator*)

**The making of a movie is a complex division of labour, involving many specialist skills brought together at the right time, place and cost. *Gladiator* features armies locked in battle but the making of the film required intensive planning and collaboration in the manner of a military operation.**

*Gladiator* grew out of conversations between screenwriter David Franzoni, and DreamWorks studio executives Walter Parkes and Laurie McDonald about the possibility of a film set in ancient Rome. Franzoni had worked for Steven Spielberg on *Amistad* (1997) so it is not surprising that the latter also responded positively. Franzoni's pitch to him went thus: 'Dodger Stadium with swords' (i.e. part modern, reflecting the modern sports spectacle, and part ancient history). He had been inspired by Daniel Mannix's 1958 novel *Those About to Die*.

DreamWorks producer Walter Parkes then took the idea to the experienced British film director Ridley Scott whose interest he aroused partly by showing him the painting Pollice Verso ('Thumbs Down') by nineteenth century French artist Jean-Léon Gérôme (viewable at www.batguano.com/bgma/GERgladB.jpg). Scott was hooked by its image of both Roman glory and wickedness. He also welcomed the challenge of reviving a genre that had fallen from favour.

## The package

A spectacular epic movie like *Gladiator* was particularly dependent on the size of its budget, unlike, say, a small-scale comedy of manners or psychological drama. In this case, it was $103 million. There would be further costs, notably the making of prints and marketing. To recoup that investment, *Gladiator* would have to gross roughly $150 million before it started making money.

Clearly careful planning and control over spending would be the order of the day. Thus costumes and props like weaponry and chariots were made for the film by carpenters and other crew rather than hired since it promised to (and did) save money. However, film economics are very vulnerable to unforeseen events. In the case of *Gladiator*, just two extra minutes of film to replace the dead Oliver Reed cost £2 million.

*Gladiator* was risky business, given the omens from the commercial failure of similar epics in the 1960s. A package is likely to be 'green-lit' if those putting it together have got a proven track record in producing box office hits. The producer, Douglas Wick, had just made the children's book *Stuart Little* (1999) into a $140m hit. The executive producer Walter Parkes had overseen successful films like *American Beauty* (1999) and *Saving Private Ryan*. Parkes in turn was also the co-head of DreamWorks pictures, jointly owned by Steven Spielberg. It was to be the source of much of the finance.

Part of the package is the product itself. *Gladiator*'s makers opted to create a straight historical epic. This might seem the only way to treat ancient Rome. But one should not forget films like the British 60s comedy movie *Carry On Cleo* (1964) or BBC TV's very popular *Up Pompeii* sitcom. Fellini's *Satyricon* (1969) was a visual extravagance that emphasised the hedonistic decadence of Roman civilisation. Films like *Kelly's Heroes* (1970) indulged in almost comic book violence in their treatments of military combat.

The success of several films such as Kevin Cosner's *Dances With Wolves* and Clint Eastwood's *Unforgiven* (1992) spotlighted that there was still a market for what might be called a 'good, honest, traditional movie'. Things are kept pretty straight-faced. The focus remains firmly on action, not dwelling on the politics of ancient Rome. Here it follows Mel Gibson's *Braveheart* which largely concentrated on the derring-do, ignoring the complexities of rival claims to the Scottish throne or the economics of feudalism.

To avoid censorship problems, the violence depicted is comparatively restrained. There are glimpses of heads and limbs being severed or crushed to pulp but, generally, blood and gore are kept in the shadows or at a tasteful distance. Similarly, only the feet of the burned bodies of Maximus' family are shown, the camera focused on Maximus, not the horror he is supposedly seeing. Perhaps modern tastes are too fastidious for the film to have depicted the incredible quantity of animals slaughtered in the real Roman games. Sex simply fails to raise its head.

## Choosing the right people

One of the most crucial choices is that of film director. The film was firmly aimed at the multiplex market and had a correspondingly big budget. It might seem a bit surprising that Ridley Scott was chosen given that some of his films in the 1990s (*1492: Conquest Of Paradise*, *White Squall* and *G.I. Jane*) had not been box office successes. On the other hand, the financial success of *Alien* (1979) had given Scott much credit at the bank while *Blade Runner* (1982) had won him great esteem in the eyes of many movie buffs and critics.

Perhaps Scott's image in Hollywood was captured by a remark made by Jerry Bruckheimer, one of Hollywood's leading producers and in many ways 'king' of the modern blockbuster. He produced another of Scott's films, *Black Hawk Down* (2002). He referred to it as the closest he had come to an 'art house' movie.

That might seem a strange description if the film were to be compared to films usually associated with non-mainstream movie-making. Yet it does suggest that Scott was trusted to be able to bring certain special cinematic qualities to his films, the kind of things critics and fans alike value in *Alien* and *Blade Runner* — rich mise-en-scène and masterly camerawork. These would be the very things that might extend the appeal of *Gladiator* beyond the numerous but still limited ranks of action film fans.

## Cast

Casting decisions can be crucial. Several stories surround the choices for *Gladiator*. Indeed, this kind of rumour-mill can part of the overall publicity for a movie. It was rumoured that Mel Gibson was a possible Maximus (on the lines of the wronged heroes of *Braveheart* and *The Patriot* (2000)). Apparently, Jude Law was considered for Commodus, Nicole Kidman for Lucilla and Sean Connery for Marcus Aurelius.

The impact of the actual choices is discussed later under the section 'Responses to *Gladiator*'. Here, it might be remembered that there have been many successful movies with unknown casts (as with the early French New Wave and many 'indie' films). Yet there remained the danger that fewer people might be drawn to see a film lacking 'big names'.

The character of Maximus is centre stage for most of the film, giving its casting special importance. Russell Crowe offered particularly appropriate qualities, not least an especially strong physical presence on the screen, steely eyes and an aura of dignity. The fact that he was not an overexposed top actor might have been a strength. As producer Douglas Wick put it, 'you really want to believe that Maximus is a real person and not a movie star in a toga'.

Crowe's membership of the rock band Thirty Odd Foot of Grunts might have given him and therefore the film extra appeal in certain younger parts of the possible audience. He had also appeared in the soap opera *Neighbours*, memories of which might add to the potential audience.

Joaquin Phoenix also brought to Commodus suitably odious qualities but also a certain vulnerability. The fact that his dead brother River Phoenix had gained a certain cult status

and that Joaquin himself is well-known in animal rights' circles promised to further build the audience for *Gladiator*.

The film did not employ glamorous actresses like Julia Roberts, Cameron Diaz, Halle Berry or Jennifer Lopez. They would not only have been more expensive but could have unbalanced the film. Connie Nielsen had played opposite Al Pacino in *The Devil's Advocate* (1997), her breakthrough role. Presumably her looks promised to catch the gaze of many men in the audience. At the same time, she could plausibly play the part of a concerned mother.

Other members of the cast came from an older stable of actors, notably Richard Harris, Derek Jacobi, David Hemmings and Oliver Reed, who might help to attract older sections of the cinema-going public, both in Britain and in the USA. In the latter case, such British and Irish actors often seem to enjoy extra popularity, not least for their 'thespian' qualities.

Casting decisions also reflect the industry's internal networks. Djimon Hounsou (Juba) had appeared as Cinque in Spielberg's *Amistad*, Tomas Arana (Quintus) had co-starred with Russell Crowe in *L.A. Confidential* (1997), while Joaquin Phoenix had starred the 1998 film *Clay Pigeons* which Ridley Scott had co-produced and his brother Tony executive-produced.

## From words to images and sounds

*Gladiator* illustrates the extent to which a film is a dynamic project evolving as the production advances. David Franzoni's original idea for *Gladiator* had to be turned into a shooting script. His original screenplay was severely pruned following criticism of the first draft. It was then rebuilt around the core idea (Roman general's downfall and the ensuing search for revenge). This was done by screenwriters John Logan and Bill Nicholson, with input from the

film's producer Wick and executive producers Parkes and McDonald.

Many of the changes to the original Franzoni screenplay followed. The death of Marcus Aurelius did not originally happen, for example, while the hero (and family) survived the end of the film. By contrast, Lucilla died a horrible death. Other changes were made after the first rewrite. For example, Maximus still survived. Indeed, he is seen leading the army back into Rome. Poor Lucilla still died but in the manner of the early action films, Maximus rode to the rescue of young Lucius. Commodus was killed by Maximus beneath the Colosseum, not in the actual arena. Lucius was duly adopted by the conquering hero and a happy ending ensued.

In the final version of the script, Maximus (originally called Narcissus) changed from being a father of daughters to having only one son. Maximus' future ally Juba was originally also a commander of the archers and was similarly banished to the gladiatorial arena. However, it was decided that they would meet as slaves.

Final touches took place just before a shoot took place. In particular, the opening and closing scenes were late additions. Thus Maximus became a doomed hero, giving the film greater emotional weight. Editing too can change the story. In this case, more reference was added to Maximus' family, making the character's behaviour more plausible. The more serous tone and much greater emphasis on the theme of life and death (as in Maximus' speech to his cavalry) were due to Scott's intervention.

'Gurus' of screenplay construction such as Syd Field and Michael Hauge argue that its opening pages must grab the reader and subsequent viewer emotionally. *Gladiator* certainly follows that template, giving a forceful presentation of Maximus among his men. It also creates a sense of mystery via the prologue of an unknown figure walking

**NOTES:**

through a field of wheat (in the screenplay he is identified as Maximus but this is not clear to viewers). Hauge's stress on the desirability of an unusual and interesting setting is also satisfied by the title card saying 'Germania AD 180'.

The character with whom the audience is expected to identify is introduced straightaway, another key tactic according to Hauge. However, given the need for a gripping opening battle scene, the hero's nemesis, Commodus, is not introduced until later (though immediately after the battle scene is completed). He also brings the romantic interest, Lucilla, with him.

Film-making thus combines careful planning with a degree of spontaneous improvisation. Many of these changes were made by Scott himself, something that adds weight to the auteur perspective. Other elements came about by chance, including the gesture of rubbing hands in the soil, something that Crowe just happened to do on set.

Sometimes, unpredictable events force changes. Apparently, the ending of the film was meant to include shots of Proximo signifying that his encounter with Maximus had left him a changed man. The death of actor Oliver Reed, however, forced that plan to be dropped. It is yet another reminder of the inherent unpredictability of major film productions and attendant financial risks involved (plus still further incentives to play 'safe').

## Influences

In the choice of specific images and sounds, people like the director, set designer(s), cinematographer and score composer will bring their individual imaginations to the task. Of course, various influences will be at work on their thinking such as past films. David Franzoni was quite influenced by Federico Fellini's 1969 film *Satyricon*. The scene of the arrival of Commodus in Rome and other ceremonial scenes surely owes something to Leni Riefenstahl's paean to Hitler, *Triumph of the Will* (1935). Historical epics from the hands of Cecil B. DeMille onwards have created a reservoir of ideas. The fate of Maximus' family has visual similarities with that of *Spartacus* who was nailed to a crucifix in the eponymous film.

But there may be many other sources of inspiration. The iconography of the painting 'Thumbs Down' has been mentioned already. Other inspirational paintings may have included Alma-Tadema's 'The Pyrrhic Victory' (a Spartan war dance,) Delacroix's 'The Last Words of Marcus Aurelius', Couture's 'Romans of the Decadence' and de la Tour's 'Spring Processional' and 'Banquet of Rome' (possibly the source of the idea of cascading flowers at the end of the film). Roman archaeological sites (including the triumphal columns on which scenes of battle were carved) provided more inspiration. On one, rain suddenly falls on the battlefield just as snow descends at the end of the battle with the Germanic horde.

The opening battle between the Roman army and Germanic tribesmen seems heavily influenced by the Omaha Beach scene in *Saving Private Ryan*. One might compare the progress of Captain Miller (Tom Hanks) through the action with that of Maximus, once the latter is on foot. The weaponry is very different but the physical feel of the two scenes is quite similar.

But *Gladiator* reflects other styles too. Given that Ridley Scott originally worked in advertising, it is not surprising that some of that experience, not least the emphasis on short, sharp visuals, was brought to his films. A close cousin of the TV advert is the pop video, the two blended into one on MTV. Its look is dominated by a plethora of close-ups, zooms, sudden slow motion, exaggerated sound and rapid editing, all of which characterise the action scenes of *Gladiator*.

It would be wrong, however, to conclude that the film is just a product of some 'MTV-era' of film-making. The opening battle is indeed visually striking for reasons just listed, but this is not achieved at the expense of the narrative. The camerawork and editing carefully pick out the significant figure of Marcus Aurelius, for example, just as they emphasise the affection Maximus commands from his troops as well as spotlight the disaffection of his deputy, Quintus.

## On Location

*Gladiator* was largely filmed far away from 'Tinsel Town', i.e. the place where the decision to make the movie was taken. Ancient Rome was rebuilt in Malta; the battles in Germania were staged in a Forestry Commission plantation in Surrey in southern England; the gladiator school and associated arenas were constructed in Morocco. Such choices involve a variety of considerations, not just economic but technical (in terms of locally available skills and facilities), logistical (movement of filming equipment, catering, and so forth), legal (permission to film, etc.) and possibly even political (dealings with local governmental bodies and politicians plus any political statements that might be made by using certain localities) as well as health and safety considerations (this is a film that used very real tigers).

Shooting was planned in sequence with core staff working first in Britain at the beginning of February 1999. Just over three weeks later, production moved to Morocco. Some idea of the planning involved is given by the fact that construction work there had started in December 1998, some two months ahead of shooting. By mid-March filming there had finished so production could then shift to Malta (Roman scenes) where work on sets had started 19 weeks before. Work on Malta concluded at the end of May 1999 and a short shoot in Tuscany followed (the villa of Maximus and his family)

The one element least amenable to planning is the weather. Overall climates might be fairly predictable, which was one of the attractions of

**NOTES:**

dry and sunny California in the early days of film. But even sunnier climes can suffer from inclement bad weather as did Malta during the shooting of **Gladiator**. It caused costly delays as well as expensive damage to the sets.

The filming of the battle scene required not just meticulous planning and safe use of pyrotechnics and other special effects. Too much time devoted to people simply hacking at each other might also become repetitive. Scott was therefore careful to add variety, with catapult bombardments, showers of arrows, exploding fireballs and cavalry charges. By contrast, the equivalent battle scene in **The Fall of the Roman Empire** seems to have failed to ignite audience emotions.

The scene also illustrates the possible tensions between logistical necessity and historical reality. In actuality, the archers would have been placed ahead of the infantry before firing their arrows. This would eliminate the danger of hitting their own troops. In the film, they are placed behind, firing over the infantry's heads. However, this inaccuracy would have reduced the need for complicated and time-consuming manoeuvring of extras on location. History also conflicts with other filmic needs. In real life Commodus' face would have been encased in a protective helmet when he fought in the arena. But the movie audience is likely to enjoy a film more when they see the combatants.

## Devices

Film is inherently a technological activity. A modern large-scale epic like **Gladiator** is even more dependent on technology: its use of computer-generated images understandably attracting much attention. Such computer effects came courtesy of post-production facilities at Ridley Scott's company The Mill, located in Shepperton in London's suburbs.

The (re-)creation of the Colosseum illustrates what was achieved. CGI was employed to finish the circumference of the first tier of an old Maltese fort, before adding second and third tiers to the structure, plus other features such as statues. The number of actual people present was multiplied tenfold digitally, creating a crowd of some 30,000. Crowds in the streets were similarly augmented.

CGI was also used to extend other sets created in Malta, including the Emperor's palace, the forum, the senate, the marketplace of Rome, the residence of Senator Gracchus and other backdrops. It was also the means by which the viewer sees otherwise impossible sights such as the sweeping vistas of ancient Rome. Yet, CGI is only one way of many in which a film will deploy an array of technological devices.

The opening battle scene illustrates the range of gadgetry and techniques employed. For instance, the audience is pitched in the drama of attacking cavalry by the device of a little monorail which allowed the camera to follow the charge through the woods. Some stunning moments depend on quite old-fashioned techniques. Maximus' encounter with live tigers continues a tradition that could be traced back to the 1913 Italian film **Quo Vadis**, which featured lions as well as a crowd of 5,000 extras (one was actually eaten by a lion!). Some effects depend on actions performed by stuntmen. Stunts not only include humans but also animals. The cavalry charge against the rear of the barbarian army obviously required horses … and, of course horse wranglers.

## Cut!

Film production involves choices about what not to film as well as what to film. It also results in the omission of footage that was filmed during the editing process as the available material, filmed in different times and places, is assembled into one work, whose sequences on screen might be quite different to those of its making.

Missing, for example, is footage of Maximus in the army hospital after the battle. This omission allows a sharper contrast to be created between its carnage and the feast, where we see (non-combatant) Marcus Aurelius, Commodus, Lucilla and the senators celebrating a victory won by others' blood and suffering. Also cut was a scene of Commodus hacking to pieces a bust of father. His violent jealousy and resentment perhaps needed no underlining. Missing too is a scene in which Commodus orders the execution of two Praetorian guards to test the loyalty of Quintus.

At one stage, it seems that Maximus would have been shown watching Christians about to be fed to lions in the arena. Its omission apparently is due to Scott's feelings that it might unbalance the story. The attention of the audience is thereby firmly kept on Maximus and his fate. Perhaps the same thinking led to the omission of a scene from the second screenplay in which Commodus is shown arresting various senators, scholars and other suspected opponents.

Sometimes financial considerations dictate the choices. One decision was not to do a scene in which Maximus was to train with a rhino. Apparently it would have added $3 million to the costs. Perhaps more startling is the way certain things were not left out on the grounds of their implausibility when in fact they would have been perfectly realistic. A scene was dropped in which Maximus would have been seen endorsing products like olive oil, which did happen in real life. Film 'realism' and historical reality thus diverge once more.

**NOTES:**

# Building an Audience for *Gladiator*

A man for all seasons

**'Win the crowd'** (Proximo in *Gladiator*)

**Mainstream movies are made to appeal to large audiences. However, as the novelist and film scriptwriter William Goldman once remarked, 'nobody knows anything' in the film industry. The heart of the problem is the volatility of public tastes and the resultant risk that money invested in a movie may never be recouped.**

It is a problem that has grown worse in recent decades. The costs of mainstream blockbusters have gone up while audiences have become more fickle, not least due to the proliferation of rival sources of entertainment. Sometimes, studios have a surprise hit on their hands but then follow-ups from the same directors and/or stars do badly at the box office. Sometimes, no amount of smart marketing will save a film. There seems to be no accounting for public taste.

Though cinema-going has enjoyed a general revival in popularity, the recovery is quite shaky. Thus in the first six months of 2003, audiences in Britain were lower than in the same period of 2002. For such reasons, there is even greater pressure to broaden the possible appeal of a film. It is not just a matter of audience numbers in a purely quantitative sense. Rather, in a society that seems to be fragmenting into all kinds of sub-groups, profitable films are most likely to be ones that appeal across a range of different audience segments.

Audiences could be divided in terms of not just more traditional classifications such as gender, ethnicity and age but also ones based more on lifestyle and beliefs. This is a major change compared to the more socially homogenous world of, say, 50 years ago. This change clearly complicates any assessment by the movie business of who might like what films.

It is worth stressing here just how 'knowing' modern film audiences have become. Before the 1960s, audiences usually got to see films only at the time of their release. Television transformed this situation. Thereafter, audiences might watch new movies by going to the cinema but also see old ones they missed or were too young to see first time round as well as watch again movies they had seen already by simply turning on the television set at home. The advent of video then DVD deepened this process.

The frequency with which shows like *The Simpsons* make references to a whole range of movies suggests that many young people, as well as older generations of film fans, know a lot about film. The explosive growth in the number of film courses at colleges and universities has also encouraged wider knowledge of old movies.

## Possible audiences

The average age of the cinema-goer has dramatically fallen since the peak of audience attendances back in 1946. The core target audience for a film playing at the multiplexes is likely to be 15–25, with, in the case of action blockbusters, a bias towards young men. Cinema-goers today are not very different to the kind of characters seen in films whose names seem to be a variation of 'Porky Knows What You Did Last Summer in American Pie High School 3', which is why so many films of this type get made.

According to the American Motion Picture Association, young and frequent movie-goers represent the majority of admissions in the USA. In particular, though the 12–29 age group makes up some 30% of the general US population, it constitutes almost half of annual cinema admissions. Frequent movie-goers make up 78% of total admissions.

But there are other parts of the potential total audience at whom a film might be aimed. Although many older adults never go to the cinema, there are still quite a few exceptions to that rule, as the success of such 'old-fashioned' films like *Gosford Park* (2001) suggest. Someone who, at the age of 15, enjoyed *Ben-Hur* on its first release, would only be 66 when *Gladiator* arrived, a comparative 'spring chicken' in our ageing society and perhaps be tempted to see what a modern epic looks like.

In fact, there have been significant increases in movie-going among the 40–59 age group. The number of movie-goers in the 12–24 age group has remained constant since 2001 but there has been an increase of 2.1% among those aged 50+ during the same period. British figures, quoted by King (2002) show a similar trend, though it should be stressed that what might seem a drastic rise in percentage terms (450% increase in people over 45 going to UK cinemas during the 1990s) might be quantitatively less dramatic in absolute terms since it was based on small numbers in the first place.

In the light of such figures it would seem sensible to make some movies in a given year's batch which could offer something to those older parts of the market as well as more

**NOTES:**

# Building an Audience for *Gladiator*

youthful cinema-goers. **Gladiator** would seem a well conceived vehicle to achieve that aim. It offers something for teenagers, their parents and possibly grandparents too. It has action but also characters who, though not developed in depth, are not simply one-dimensional. It has a strong back story and employs, alongside a rising younger star, a number of veteran actors familiar to older sections of the audience. Above all, it has Rome, which, as will be discussed below, seems to exercice a peculiar fascination for all age groups.

The pressure to broaden audience numbers often comes at the expense of aesthetic quality. Risqué subject matter, controversial opinions, experimental camerawork and so forth might well be sacrificed to avoid giving offence. The film might also be compromised by the presence of incompatible ingredients stirred into the mix in the hope of pulling in a few more viewers. This dynamic can be seen in **Gladiator**'s rather schizophrenic characterisation of its hero. On one hand, he's the rough and tough general, more than ready to kill over and over again (something for the lads!), yet he's a gentle soul who simply wants to return to his family and plant his fields (something for the ladies!).

## Sales pitch

It is one thing to work into a movie all kinds of possible appeal in order to build an audience for it. Financial success also depends upon a careful campaign of publicity and marketing to translate potential cinema-goers into actual box office sales.

There are exceptions whereby a film can attract audiences by other means, notably clever use of the Internet as in the case of **The Blair Witch Project**. It remains the case that word-of-mouth recommendations remain the primary means by which people are persuaded to go and see a film. None the less, in the case of films like **Gladiator**, firmly aimed at the multiplex market, a large part of the overall budget will be spent on persuading people that

it is a 'must-see' movie. So while the production budget was $103 million, the advertising budget was $42.7 million (this figure did also include the cost of making prints).

A distinction must be made between publicity and marketing. The former is being used in the sense of coverage of the film in the media for which the film distributors make no payments. It might take the form of reports about problems experienced during production or of interviews given by the director and the film's stars in the press or on TV and radio chat shows. Thus Joaquin Phoenix duly appeared in May 2000 on both *Late Night with David Letterman* and *The Tonight Show with Jay Leno* promoting **Gladiator**. Even seemingly 'negative' items can make audiences more aware of a film and raise their curiosity. Press stories about Russell Crowe's anti-social behaviour in Malta and Morocco probably did no harm, no matter how irritating he might have been for local people.

Actual reviews of the film are another kind of publicity. In turn, marketing tools like posters and advertisements in the press might make use of favourable comments from the critics (sometimes rather selectively). Indeed it is possible, especially in the broadsheets, to read a hostile review by the resident critic next to an advertisement featuring endorsements from a fellow critic extolling its virtues.

It is increasingly common to see 'Making of…' documentaries on TV, especially in the case of special effects blockbusters. These tend to be somewhat uncritical, little more than advertising 'puffs' for the films as well as comparatively cheap fillers of the TV schedules. More dangerously, today's films are vulnerable to adverse criticism on the Internet. After **Gladiator**'s preview screening in San Diego, reviews were posted on websites that night (fortunately for the film they were positive). Spoilers from such sources may negatively affect audiences as well.

## Promotion

The term 'marketing' is best used to describe those activities financed by the distributors to attract an audience for their film. The budget to do all this is normally around 33% of estimated gross. It includes such familiar things as film trailers in the cinema and on TV as well as one or more posters. But it can include adverts on the side of buses and taxis, preview 'talker screenings' (in the hope that those who get to see a film for free then recommend it to others), special first night offers and special opening galas. Press packs are distributed to 'help' reviewers and other journalists form a positive opinion of a film (not least by making their job easier).

In the case of films which first went on release in the USA before being screened abroad, there is the extra possibility of using American box office figures (or, rather, successful ones) to persuade foreign audiences that the film has already pleased lots of people. Sometimes the campaign will be carried out in stages, with a set of trailers and/or posters 'teasing' the audience as they gradually reveal more and more about the film (the marketing of **Independence Day** remains a classic example).

Merchandising of spin-off products and tie-in deals also figure prominently in the choices made by the film's distributors. This is an increasingly important source of income (at times greater than box office receipts) as well as an additional form of publicity, both for the film and for companies signing 'tie-in' deals (often fast food outlets). Merchandising is nothing if not varied, including all sorts of toys, computer games, clothes, lunch boxes, luggage as well as assorted print by-products such as 'Making of…' books and the 'rejacketing' of adapted novels. In some cases, money will be made from product placement from cola drinks to computers in films. Of course, both licensees of spin-off products and firms paying to have their product placed in the film will have a vested interest in the film's success.

**NOTES:**

## On message

The marketing campaign will explore all possible points of appeal and selectively pitch them to specific audiences by whatever means will reach them (and ideally no one else) in the most cost effective way. There is no point in buying a TV slot in the middle of, say, *Coronation Street*. Not only would it be very expensive but the reached audience would include many people unlikely to even consider going to the cinema.

Having identified how to reach the desired audience, the selection of the precise message is the next choice. The DVD of **Independence Day**, for example, includes the advert broadcast on MTV which made the movie look like a joke-ridden action burlesque, playing down the straight sci-fi elements. Presumably, it was assumed that MTV viewers only like crass comedies.

It is quite common in fact for different messages to be aimed at different sections of the film-going public as confirmed by interviews conducted with **Gladiator**'s distributors by King (2002). Adverts placed on TV in the middle of sports programmes emphasised the action side of the film. However, ones broadcast with shows like *Ally McBeal* stressed more personal elements (Maximus' loss of his family, his anguish and desire for vengeance).

That said, the posters most certainly did not feature compositions of Maximus and Lucilla, in the manner of those for, say, **Braveheart** or **Last of the Mohicans** (1992), both of which included the 'love interest'. Actually the **Gladiator** posters, with the dominant image of a brooding Russell Crowe, actually do sell the 'goods' accurately — the film is nothing without Maximus.

## Selling Point

**Gladiator** received saturation marketing. According to Deborah Sheppard, UIP Director of Marketing, the distributors 'put all (the) advertising behind one date. We spent a lot of money ensuring nobody could move without knowing about it' (quoted in Macnab, 2000). Within the various marketing products, there are a number of different options. The very name of a film can be a marketing tool. **Gladiator** is simply one strong word that instantly gives a clue to the film's setting and perhaps even its storyline. Other films might, of course, have titles that are deliberately obscure, if not misleading.

Most film marketing material will contain taglines that provide similar incentives to see the film. **Gladiator** had several: 'What We Do In Life Echoes In Eternity'; 'A Hero Will Rise'; 'The Gladiator Who Defied An Empire'; 'The Gladiator Who Defied An Emperor'; 'The General Who Became A Slave'; 'The Slave Who Became A Gladiator'; 'Some Sought Glory, Fame And Honour. He Came For Revenge'; 'In This Life Or The Next, I Will Have My Vengeance'; 'Strength And Honour!'; 'Are You Not Entertained?'; 'Death Smiles At Us All'; and 'A Slave Who Controlled An Empire'. Together they give a good idea of both the film's genre and its narrative.

The movie's genre might be used to market it if similar films or comparable texts in other media are proving to be popular. Despite the long absence of biblical and Roman epics from the cinema screen, the posters and trailers for **Gladiator** proudly displayed what was on offer. History as a subject had undergone something of a resurgence across all media so it would appear to have been a wise choice to spotlight what the film was about.

Some films proclaim the name of their director. Not surprisingly, Steven Spielberg often gets a mention even when he had only the slightest connection to the film. More often it is the presence of certain stars that is spotlighted. Sometimes just one person is singled out, at other times (particularly when there are no 'big names') several leading actors get a mention (in the case of **Gladiator**, there were some posters with images of Russell Crowe, sword in hand, with his name in smaller point size about the title of the film).

Others, however, just featured a tagline ('A Hero Will Arise') with the movie's name, presumably on the grounds that at the time Crowe did not have the star status of, say, Tom Hanks or Tom Cruise. Most featured stormy, almost fiery clouds in the background, sometimes with the ruins of the Colosseum visible, giving a strong feel of violent action on offer.

One option not really open to the distributors of **Gladiator** was the strategy of linking the film to the 'spirit' of the times or zeitgeist. This is a very elusive quality and perhaps one which cannot be planned. But it does happen. Examples include 50s teenage 'angst' and **Rebel Without A Cause** (1955), the emergent Disco scene and **Saturday Night Fever** (1977), and an 'anti-everything' nihilism and **Trainspotting** (1996). The marketing of **Gladiator**, by contrast, took a stand on rather more solid ground. It offered straight down-the-line entertainment, soaked with spectacular action scenes and amazing reconstructions of ancient Rome, through a good old-fashioned hero who would do his duty.

**Gladiator** had, however, one significant advantage compared to other blockbusters. It was a product that was comparatively easy to differentiate. By contrast films with a more familiar mix of big stars, car chases, crude comedy and special effects wizardry (**Speed 2** (1997), **Twister**, **Con Air**, **Space Jam** (1996), **Armageddon** and **Godzilla**) have even more need of clever advertising campaigns to help them stand out from the crowd and even then, as in **Godzilla**, it does not always work.

Marketing resumes when a film starts a new

**NOTES:**

# Building an Audience for *Gladiator*

'life' via cable, satellite and terrestrial TV as well as video and DVD. FOXTEL had competitions offering a 'full Gladiator experience', with a free trip to Rome. Logos promoted 'Gladiator Month Dec. 2001 AD'. The world of advertising is even less a stickler for historical accuracy than the film industry itself. One advertisement for the screening on Sky TV read 'Born Wellington 1964. Died Rome 100 BC', an error of 280 years in the case of the film's setting. As can also be seen from this tagline, Russell Crowe had become more central in the TV sales pitch, in this case with the heading 'Crowe-Maximus'.

## Time and place

Last but not least comes a series of choices about where and when a film is to be first screened. There are obvious advantages to holiday seasons for films aspiring to be big box office successes, though it must be said that the possibilities of summer releases were not fully appreciated by the film industry until the stunning success of *Jaws* in June 1975.

Weekends have evident significance as non-work or non-school days and none more so than the opening weekend for a film. Indeed it is now a real litmus test of a film's potential, largely due to the capacity of computerised systems to speedily collect and process data about attendance. High figures will add to a film's appeal by making it seem a 'must-see' movie. It is here that word-of-mouth really plays a crucial part in a film's fortunes.

Choice will be also influenced by what other rival films may be due for release. The screening of fairly similar films, be it about incoming asteroids or animated bugs, is not necessarily something to be avoided. Their release within the same period can be used to give a sense that such films are the 'flavour of the month'. Other events such as World Cup football on TV might be a factor, sometimes encouraging the release of movies that might appeal to that part of the audience, often females, who do not share their partners'

obsession with sport.

Timing is one choice but so too is location. Some films are 'four-walled', meaning that the film is screened simultaneously in cinemas in all main centres, i.e. to the north, south, east and west, with the big blockbusters being shown on several screens at the same multiplex cinema. Sometimes premieres may be arranged so that a platform is created giving a film a better 'take-off' platform at the box office. Other films may, of course, be confined to the 'art house' cinema circuit.

*Gladiator* opened at nearly 3,000 screens in the USA on 5 May 2000. That number actually went above 3,000 during May before falling back to just over a 1,000 by the second fortnight in July. The film opened a week later in the UK on 12 May, the comparative size of the two markets being partly reflected in the fact that it opened at 417 screens on this side of the Atlantic (the British total number of screens at that time being less than the number at which just *Gladiator* was screened in the USA).

On that first weekend in the USA, the film earned $34,819,000 at the box office while in the UK the sum was £3,555,446 (very crudely this is 20% of the American takings). The significance of the first weekend is also underlined by the fact that the takings of the first weekend in July, eight weeks later, were down to $2,426,000 in the USA and £760,278 in the UK.

## Making money

It has been repeatedly stressed that a film like *Gladiator* is a commercial product. It may also be remembered that the film had cost around $103,000,000 to make, apart from the cost of prints and advertising. Now it is total earnings from all sources, including merchandising, tie-in deals, sales to TV and so forth, that will determine the eventual balance sheet of profit or loss. By the third weekend *Gladiator* had recouped its production costs in cumulative

box office takings in the USA alone. Again the crucial importance of the American market is striking but so too is *Gladiator*'s global reach. Its worldwide gross was to be $457,200,000, amply covering all its costs.

Box office takings are now just a part of a modern film's potential revenue and quite frequently less than 50% of total income. There is clearly a lot of money to be made from computer games, toys, tie-in drinks and other spin-off products. Part of the market is what is called the kidult, adults who buy what otherwise might seem childish products (for example, Shrek bottle openers, etc.). In other words, new audiences/consumers can be built upon those attracted to cinemas themselves.

*Gladiator* cannot be compared to films like *Stars Wars* and other merchandising extravaganza. Its merchandising possibilities (licensed by Universal Studios Consumer Products group) obviously could not match a film like *Shrek* (2001) whose very nature lends itself to a myriad tie-in products. Most income beyond box office takings would come from video and DVD releases as well as sales to network, satellite and cable TV.

## TV arena

Non-cinema audiences should not be underestimated. Apparently a majority of Americans now have never been to a cinema. Yet film as a form remains highly popular. Witness the proliferation of TV channels based on the screening of movies as well as the emergence of the high spending DVD buyers (according to *Billboard* 50% of these in America are women, perhaps a surprising figure). Clearly an expensive movie like *Gladiator* must tap into these additional markets.

King (2002) speculates that the film was made in ways that would suit television, not just cinema screens. He notes how the big battle in *Spartacus* on a big open plain, with lots of aerial long shots, almost demands cinema

**NOTES:**

whereas much of the action in **Gladiator** is comparatively close quarter and can be rendered reasonably well on a small screen. It also has many moments of political intrigue (the Emperor and his son, the senators, etc.) and even semi-romantic exchanges (Maximus and Lucilla) all of which do not need big screens.

**Gladiator** followed the conventional pattern of distribution and subsequent follow-on products. Seven months after its theatrical release, the DVD and video versions went on sale in November 2000. To build DVD sales, various extras were added to the film itself, ranging from deleted scenes to background documentaries. Globally, some 4.5 million DVDs were sold, a record at that time. Obviously these releases were timed to capture the Christmas present-buying market. The film played a significant part in raising industry awareness of the market represented by DVD.

TV viewers are another audience (though, of course, they include some who saw the film in the cinema). In April 2001, the film premiered on British TV on the pay-per-view cable network Front Row who clearly used the film in its battle with rival Sky Box Office. In October that year the film made its satellite debut in Britain on Sky Premier. Its aural qualities were exploited to stress the benefits of going over to Sky and its newly introduced Dolby Digital 5:1.

Terrestrial broadcasts followed two years later in 2003, a gap that reflects the key role that movies play in maintaining satellite subscriptions. Channel 5 won a hotly contested fight for the first screening. These deals were 'non-exclusive', leaving Universal to pursue further sales. The possibility of bidding for **Gladiator** objects like swords was used to launch Sky's Auction World.

An official illustrated companion book for **Gladiator** was published in the USA by Newmarket Pictorial Moviebooks. It was written by John Logan and David Franzoni, featuring excerpts from the screenplay, historical sidebars, illustrations, details on period costumes and set designs, behind-the-scenes photographs from the location plus interviews with the screenwriters, actors and director. Others also rode on the back of **Gladiator**, including Daniel Mannix, the author of the novel that had originally inspired **Gladiator** screenplay writer David Franzoni, *Those About to Die* (see his *Way of the Gladiator*, 2001).

The soundtrack CD seems to have been the most successful piece of merchandise directly linked to the film. It tapped two markets in particular. One was that for so-called 'ambient music' (i.e. ethereal sounds to which people might 'chill out'), which Lisa Gerrard's vocal contributions to the score suited. The success of groups like Clannad had demonstrated its appeal. Another strong market is that for ethnic sounds and 'world music', again something that the instrumentation of the score matches. Spanish guitar, Chinese dulcimer and Armenian duduk are all featured, for example.

A successful film may also create a market for consumer products tapping into the same thematic matter. There is a computer game, *Gladiator: Sword of Vengeance*, which has a very similar storyline to the movie though the characters are changed. Lucasarts also released the game *Gladius*. It might be noted that this market is just as volatile as film-making, with Acclaim, makers of the first game, going bankrupt in 2004.

**NOTES:**

# 'Auteur Theory' and *Gladiator*

Star and director

**'What possible difference can I make?'**
(Maximus in *Gladiator*)

**Across the top of the cover of the DVD of**
*Gladiator* **run four words: 'A Ridley Scott**
**Film'. That seemingly simple statement**
**actually poses a major question about the**
**creative process by which movies get made**
**and about what distinguishes one group of**
**films from another. One answer focuses on**
**the people who make movies and especially**
**the film director.**

This is an obvious approach when it comes to
the composition of music, the writing of a
novel, play or poem, the creation of a painting,
sculpture and so forth. In such cases, it seems
self-evident that individual composers, authors,
painters, sculptors or some other artists were
the driving creative force, putting their
personal 'stamp' on their creation.

In the case of film, the term 'auteur theory' has
been given to the parallel approach in film
analysis ('auteur' is French for 'author'). Usually
it is the film's director who is singled out to be
the equivalent to composers and the like. Auteur
theory does not necessarily displace genre
analysis. Thus, films like ***Stagecoach*** (1939),

*Colorado Territory* (1949), ***Bend of the River***
(1952), ***Rio Bravo*** (1959), ***The Wild Bunch***
(1969) and ***A Fistful of Dollars*** (1964) share
similar ingredients, one which most viewers
would describe as conventions of the western
(genre theory) yet they are also different to each
other while sharing certain characteristics with
other films from other genres made by the same
director (respectively John Ford, Howard
Hawks, Raoul Walsh, Anthony Mann, Sam
Peckinpah and Sergio Leone).

As the word 'auteur' itself suggests, this theory first
flowered in France. The sudden influx of many
American movies after the end of the German
occupation in World War II led some critics there
to perceive certain similarities between films from
the same director, as if he (and it was mainly 'he')
was doing with the camera what authors do with
the pen. Indeed, the film theorist Alexandre
Astruc chose to call his influential 1948 essay 'Le
Caméra-stylo' (i.e. camera-pen).

Some theorists went even further. Attacking older
film-makers for a lack of individuality in their
films, they decided to make movies themselves,
ones which would very much bear their own
mark. Perhaps the best example was François

Truffaut, a leading director in the 'French New
Wave' of the early 1960s, a movement in which
other directors similarly sought to do 'their own
thing' (Jean-Luc Godard, etc.).

This very personal approach was to be echoed
elsewhere, not least among the so-called 'movie
brats' of the New Hollywood that emerged in
the late 1960s and early 1970s. Perhaps the
most vocal advocate of the auteur approach
outside of France was also an American, the
critic Andrew Sarris who, in the 60s,
popularised the term 'auteur theory'.

Perhaps Alfred Hitchcock is the most well-
known film 'auteur' among the general public.
Certainly companies releasing videos and DVD
are quick to brand products with labels such as
the 'Hitchcock Collection'. Similarly magazines
like *Empire* have brought out special volumes
under the imprint of The Director's Collection
(with editions on the likes of Steven Spielberg).
Publishers like Virgin Books also produce series
such as 'The Complete…' with individual
books devoted to studies of the work of such
directors as Stanley Kubrick.

Sometimes film distributors privilege the name
of the director in their marketing material, not
least posters, on the assumption that viewers
will know — and want to see — what is in
store in the latest movie from a particular
director. In recent years, few have rivalled
Quentin Tarantino in this respect.

It is also common to see re-releases of existing
films being marketed as the 'Director's Cut',
implying that the director's original vision was
somehow mangled by the film studio. Again it
is the special status of the director that is being
exploited. It is a matter of opinion whether it is
a mere marketing ploy or a serious attempt to
give audiences the chance to see the
unblemished version of what was intended.

Thus, one can see two versions of Ridley
Scott's ***Blade Runner*** (1982, 2001), though
Sean Redmond's study of the films argues that

**NOTES:**

the so-called Director's Cut was more a commercial ploy than true rendition of Scott's original vision. Yet there are quite a few such re-releases where the restored or otherwise amended version is dramatically different as in the case of Kevin Costner's ***Dances with Wolves***, where the longer version clarifies an otherwise confused plot.

## 'I made that!'

Certain directors are, then, widely deemed worthy of 'auteur' status: these include American directors like Frank Capra, Roger Corman, Fritz Lang, David Lynch, Vincente Minnelli, Arthur Penn, Otto Preminger, George Romero, Don Siegel, Douglas Sirk and Orson Welles. Some had moved to the USA from Europe as in the case of Lang, Preminger, Sirk and the British Alfred Hitchcock (a path others have followed subsequently, including Ridley Scott).

Some British directors have also been singled out for the individuality of their work, including Terence Fisher, Mike Leigh, Ken Loach, Alexander MacKendrick, Michael Powell and Nicolas Roeg. Their ranks are swelled by a number of film-makers from outside the English-speaking world such as Sweden's Ingmar Bergman, Germany's Wim Wenders, Italy's Federico Fellini, the former Soviet Union's Sergei Eisenstein and Japan's Akira Kurosawa.

There have been cases where directors were somewhat neglected in their home country but became celebrated abroad. The American director Sam Fuller, for example, made some strikingly personal films, often based on his own experiences as a crime reporter and then World War II infantryman but gained most recognition in France for his movies. Then there is the unusual case of artists like Clint Eastwood who might be said to make their mark on movies both in front of and behind the camera.

The way auteur theory might be employed can be illustrated by the example of the ***Alien*** series of films to which a string of notable directors have contributed, namely David Fincher (***Se7en***

(1995), etc.), James Cameron (***Titanic***, etc.) and, first of all, the director of ***Gladiator***, Ridley Scott in 1979. Genre theory would direct attention to the ways these films used codes and conventions from the horror genre, into which ingredients, notably the setting and the threat from alien creatures, from science fiction have also been blended. Fincher's film (***Alien³*** (1993)) also has elements of what might called the 'prison movie' while Cameron (***Aliens*** (1986)) includes features from the war movie (platoon of rather mixed characters on a combat mission and being confronted with a seemingly invincible enemy, leading to a 'last stand').

Auteur theory, by contrast, focuses on what characteristics Fincher's film might share with, say, ***Se7en*** or ***Fight Club*** (1999). Similarly it suggests that ***Aliens*** is a 'James Cameron' film, in the same mould as ***Titanic*** and his two ***Terminator*** films. Thus, ***Gladiator*** would be deemed to be part of a distinct and coherent body of work created by Ridley Scott alongside not just ***Alien*** but also his many other films.

So far discussion has focused on the role of film directors. But it should be noted that others could be deemed 'auteurs'. There are several actors and actresses who have made a personal mark on the films in which they have appeared. ***The Shining*** (1980) may be a distinguished horror film directed by Stanley Kubrick and ***Missouri Breaks*** (1986) a western from the distinctive hand of Arthur Penn, but both are distinguished by the striking presence of Jack Nicholson.

Stars are not the only other possible film auteurs. Some film studios have had such a 'house style' that it could be said that they too 'author' movies. There is something quite distinctive, for example, about the gangster films made by Warners in the inter-war years, not least their concern for the causes of crime, not just cops and robbers. MGM musicals stand out for their high production values, especially the glossy colour sheen. There are many comedy films but those from the British

studio Ealing possess their own distinctiveness quirkiness.

***Gladiator*** was co-produced by Universal Studios who, in the 1930s, produced a string of very distinctive horror films. Yet in its more recent incarnation as part of the Universal Vivendi Group, it is hard to see any particular trademark in term of either subject matter or style. Similarly, the other production company involved, DreamWorks SKG, has not developed any particular house style.

Some films bear the mark of what might be called a 'film movement', a group of directors and other creative elements who, at a particular juncture in history, seem to be producing films with marked similarities. A well-known example is the so-called 'French New Wave' of the early 1960s while across the Channel, a group of films by different directors are often grouped together as British social realism because of their distinctively gritty, 'kitchen-sink' qualities. ***Gladiator*** cannot be said to be the product of any such movement.

Last but not least, certain countries might be said to be home of a distinctive 'national cinema'. Certainly films that came out of Japan from the 1950s onwards and from Hong Kong in more recent years are very distinctive. The same is true of so-called 'Bollywood' movies from India. There were distinctive German and Russian musicals in the 1930s. British (or perhaps rather English) comedy films might be said to bear a common tendency towards humorous understatement and self-deprecation, coupled to the more bawdy traditions of the seaside postcard.

***Gladiator*** is clearly a 'Hollywood' film but it is hard to see it as an 'American' movie. Rather, companies like Universal are part of a globalised culture straddling the planet. Though westerns and gangster films might be said to be quintessentially American genres, an American national cinema, if there is such a thing, is perhaps to be found in the thriving, though

**NOTES:**

# 'Auteur Theory' and *Gladiator*

often overlooked realm of much smaller-scale independent movie-makers (John Sayles, Kevin Smith, the Coen Brothers, Spike Lee, etc.).

None of which is intended to suggest that different ways of understanding authorship in film are incompatible. It is perfectly possible to see films as products of several authorial processes. A film like *Metropolis* (1927) might be said to be a piece of science fiction cinema ('genre') made by Fritz Lang (director-as-auteur) and part of a stylistic movement called German expressionism, reflecting the national circumstances of the time (the tensions of the Weimar Republic in Germany).

Yet, it is to the director that discussion of a film's distinctive trademarks invariably returns (partly reflected in the far greater number of studies of individual directors than, say, studios). But it is a theory whose validity can be questioned in many ways.

## What about me?

The obvious objection to the director-as-auteur theory can be seen in the credits of *Gladiator* and indeed of just about every film ever made. As the names of actors, film crew and many more roll by, films can be seen to be the work of many, many hands. While other artists and musicians may labour alone over their work, films are clearly a collective effort.

The making of a movie requires numerous people with a diversity of skills to make their input in certain sequences in a co-ordinated effort that sometimes resembles a military campaign. In such circumstances, it might be questioned whether, under such circumstances, one person can make a movie his or her personal statement. Many 'voices' are heard in a film. Screenwriters in particular often question the lead role of the director since it is their work that is the basis of the film.

If one looks at films directed by widely celebrated auteurs such as Alfred Hitchcock, it can be seen that others helped to give many of his films their particular identity. *Psycho* (1960) is a good example. It is hard to imagine the film with the input of Bernard Hermann's music or the design work of Saul Bass. It was the set designs of H. R. Giger that really made Ridley Scott's *Alien* such a striking film. The cinematography of Bruce Surtees has given many a movie directed by Clint Eastwood their distinctive style.

Then there are numerous cases where the studio heads intervened in a positive way to give a movie its final shape. The famous 'tollbooth' murder scene in Coppola's *Godfather* (1972) was added at Paramount's insistence to 'open out' the film and one would imagine that most viewers would agree with their fruit of their intervention. The 'montage' films of Sergei Eisenstein (*Battleship Potemkin* (1925), etc.) were heavily shaped both by Karl Marx's philosophical legacy and by the political context of Soviet Communism.

Auteur theory also rests on the notion of 'artistic merit'. This in turn suggests that there is some rational, even objective way of separating out real film 'artists' from the rest. Some might further suggest that it is rather pretentious to treat as somehow inferior movies that have pleased many millions in contrast to ones appreciated by only a select few. (It might be equally arrogant to reject the notion that everyone could and should learn to appreciate things they might initially neither like nor even understand.) Self-conscious 'auteurism' (i.e. personal statements in film for the sake of personal statements) might also be seen as a cult of personality, if not an egotistical self-indulgence.

It might be argued, of course, that film director is really not unlike any other worker. They turn up each day to do a specific job. It might be one requiring very special skills, not least leadership qualities. But it is still just another way of earning a living by doing what other people want. Indeed the French critics used another term to describe such activity: 'metteur-en-scène'. One wonders whether, for example, in the fourth of the *Alien* series *Alien Resurrection* (1997) Jean-Pierre Jeunet was doing a more routine piece of work, compared to his more distinctive movies like *Delicatessen* (1991) and *City of Lost Children* (1995). Actually in his book and video A Personal Journey Martin Scorsese notes that some directors do one film for the studio and one for themselves: in other words, making a living with straightforward films and making more personal statements if and when they get the chance.

Despite these and other objections to auteur theory (there are further problems with its assumption of a straight and uncomplicated link between the creator's intended vision and the audience's reception of it), it is not without some merit. Some directors (and some of the other possible auteurs discussed above) do seem to have produced a coherent body of work with distinguishing features that reflect their personal voice. Often directors have an input at other stages of a film's realisation. Ridley Scott, for example, contributed some of the sketches that were used by *Gladiator*'s conceptual artist to design a look for the film.

Perhaps directors are similar to conductors of an orchestra. Using scores written by various composers, they none the less usually tease out a united performance from the many talented individuals in front of them and sometimes do so in ways that share similar features to what they have achieved with other orchestras, playing other music and working for other impresarios.

## Ridley Scott

Ridley Scott was born in South Shields in the north-east of England in 1937. Starting work in television, Scott has produced a steady stream of films. It includes *The Duellists* (1977), *Blade Runner*, *Legend* (1985), *Someone To Watch Over Me* (1987), *Black Rain* (1987), *Thelma and Louise*, *1492: Conquest of Paradise*, *White Squall*, *G.I. Jane*, *Hannibal* (2001), *Black Hawk Down* and *Matchstick Men* (2003), a comedy caper. He remains very active with films coming off his production line, including another

**NOTES:**

historical epic ***Kingdom of Heaven*** (2005) and ***Tripoli*** announced for 2007. (For a full list of Scott's work, see www.imdb.com/name/nm0000631/)

Some of these films have been the focus for serious academic studies, notably ***Alien***, ***Blade Runner*** and ***Thelma and Louise***. ***Alien*** also enjoyed considerable popular success while ***Blade Runner*** attained definite cult status. ***Thelma and Louise*** aroused much interest as a 'road movie' with strong female protagonists. Perhaps only one of his films, ***Hannibal***, received the kind of hype usually associated with commercial blockbusters and it might also be noted in passing that some of his films, like ***Legend***, have not done well at the box office.

Scott has worked not only as a director but also film producer and writer. His early output was mainly in the field of advertising, directing more than 2,000 adverts, something that might have honed his awareness of the look of the moving image. Other family members, notably his younger brother Tony and his sons Luke and Jake are also movie-makers. Scott's contribution to movie-making as a whole earned him a knighthood in 2003.

Scott seems to have attracted a certain critical status, though some of his films have been condemned on ideological grounds by some critics. Yet it is hard to pin down what might constitute 'a Ridley Scott film'. While many people might find it comparatively easy to put into words what they associate with an Alfred Hitchcock movie (phrases like 'master of suspense' might well figure), it is probably much harder to do the same for Ridley Scott. Certainly his films as a unified body of work do not explore great themes in the manner of John Ford and his exploration of the wilderness — civilisation dichotomy in American history. Nor can he be said to have made striking innovations in the way Arthur Penn challenged the conventions of the western in his ***Little Big Man*** (1970) or the way John Carpenter pushed the horror genre in the direction of teen 'slasher' movies with his ***Halloween*** (1976).

Scott himself has provided some clues about his vision as a movie-maker. In an interview with journalist Lynn Barber, Scott describes ***Blade Runner*** as his 'most complete and personal' film. Elsewhere he has described that personal approach to movies as 'creating worlds, sometimes new worlds so I use science fiction or recreating worlds which are historical' (http://pixunlimited.co.uk/film/mov/CREATING.mov). Clearly ***Alien*** and ***Blade Runner*** fit the former bill while several commentators admired the way ***Black Hawk Down*** plunged the viewer into the world of combat, even if some objected to its ideological stance.

Fellow film-maker Alan Parker describes Scott as 'the greatest visual stylist working today' (quoted in Barber, 2002). Reading the extant material on Scott, certain words and phrases reoccur, especially ones on the lines of 'master story teller' and 'definite image maker'. One person even described Scott as 'visualcentric', a term new to this author. Certainly the look of his films is visually very rich, with his main characters often enveloped by a wealth of surrounding detail. One might study how Maximus is filmed inside the gladiatorial arena, for example, and compare it to the scenes featuring Deckard in ***Blade Runner*** or Ripley in ***Alien***.

Yet it could be said that such descriptions are simply saying that Scott is better than most at the art of directing movies but they do not necessarily qualify him as an 'auteur' in the pantheon of directors listed above. (Whether he cares or not is another matter! He is said to be worth some £60m and might feel pleased that he has provided a lot of entertainment for a lot of people in his time.)

Two other possible 'personal stamps' might be used with regard to Scott. Some of his films feature strong female characters, most obviously ***Alien*** and ***Thelma and Louise***. One is even named ***G.I. Jane***. Yet this feature is not true of his other films, especially his commercial successes like ***Gladiator***, ***Black Hawk Down*** and ***Hannibal***. It might also be argued that Scott's films are characterised by scenes of great visceral action but with little emotional depth, sophisticated characterisation or plot complexity, let alone deep political insight. But such comments could be made about many, many directors.

It should also be said that a film like ***Blade Runner*** is no simple entertainment but is a quite complex film that is both visually and intellectually rewarding. Even a comparatively minor film like ***Someone To Watch Over Me*** features quite well rounded characters (the stage villain aside). It seems rather arrogant to characterise Scott as a mere showman.

Yet Scott's films are often great shows. Perhaps, after all, it is this concern — and ability — to create alternative but plausible and engrossing worlds on the cinema screen that is the trademark of 'a Ridley Scott film'. The issue here is not whether the Roman Empire of ***Gladiator*** is really like ancient Rome (an issue discussed later). It is that viewers feel themselves convincingly transported to a battle between a Roman army and the barbarian hordes or to the arena of the Colosseum itself.

Audiences are similarly plunged into a modern urban battlefield in ***Black Hawk Down*** or find themselves in the threatening corridors and service shafts of some spacecraft of the future in ***Alien***. To take the comparatively mundane world of ***Someone To Watch Over Me***, Scott's capacity to bring to life the contrasting social spheres of a rich Manhattan socialite and an ordinary policeman and his family is still striking and distinctively so.

Ridley Scott's films might not stand out in the way of those directed by the likes of Alfred Hitchcock or John Ford, but it would be wrong to go to the other extreme and deny that ***Gladiator*** possesses no similarities with other films he has directed.

**NOTES:**

# Film Language in *Gladiator*

Emperor and General at the end of battle

'**Conjure magic for them**' (Gracchus in *Gladiator*)

**Films tell their stories via a combination of images, sounds and text on screen. Additionally, a variety of special effects can alter what is seen and heard. Selective editing of those visual and aural elements adds further possibilities to the range of filmic communication.**

In turn, audiences will draw conclusions about the time and place in which the film is set as well as the mood of both the film as a whole and particular scenes within it. They form opinions about particular characters and the relationship to each other. Generally, they will be making some sort of sense of the story as it unfolds.

Sometimes, the meanings will be obvious and just about everyone will draw the same conclusions. Often these will be the ones intended by the film-makers (hence the term 'preferred reading'). Frequently they will sense what the film is intending to communicate but go no further, taking some satisfaction from the experience but not completely (a 'negotiated reading'). On occasion, sections of the audience may reject the intended communication, as when some people laugh at what were meant to be horror films or identify with some character other than the intended hero/heroine (an 'aberrant reading').

Given the latitude with which audiences might respond to a film and possible scope for resultant confusion, film-makers often try to pin down the meaning of what is being seen and heard ('anchorage'). A common example is text on screen, often used to provide some 'back story' to the events about to happen or to specify exactly where and when the scene is taking place. Another device is a voice-over, either the thoughts apparently going on inside the head of one of the main characters or sometimes a commentary from an external narrator who possesses a seemingly omniscient awareness of the plot's development.

## Absorbed in film

Most commonly, a film's audience is positioned in the manner of people in a theatre, watching and listening to the action on the stage. Unlike the theatrical experience, there is no possibility of interaction between screen and auditorium in the cinema or a home. The audience is simply a set of onlookers though they are far from passive. Instead, they are actively interpreting and responding to the film. Some movies, usually described with words like 'non-mainstream', may be deliberately confusing or provocative. At the same time, they may try to make very clear how the film has been actually made (for example, allowing the audience to see the cameras and microphones).

Most film-makers, however, try to deliver a flow of sounds and images that will lead the audience to suspend any disbelief and, instead, immerse themselves in the film. *Gladiator* demands of its audience the willingness to believe that a victorious general could be sold into slavery, become a popular gladiator, avoid being quietly executed when no one is looking, and kill an emperor, something which never happened in history nor was ever a remote possibility.

So film language is used in ways that promise to overcome possible incredulity among its audiences. Thus, many camera shots mimic what people might actually see if they were 'there'. There will be comparatively few variations from the horizontal shot, with conversations at eye level, a modest amount of camera movement (e.g. few crash zooms and whip pans) and many shots from a medium distance, with fewer tight close-ups or extreme long shots.

Scenes are usually shot in a way that makes the 'geography' of the action clear, avoiding possible confusion about where people and things are located in relation to each other. The appearance and behaviour of characters are often contrived to seem equally plausible (larger-than-life villains and the like excepted). Lighting is similarly used to simulate reality (even if, in practice, many daytime scenes are illuminated with extra lighting).

---

**NOTES:**

*This chapter, and the opening sequence analysis in particular, is indebted to* Media and Meaning: An Introduction *(Stewart, et al, 2001). See bibliography for more details.*

Further, the editing serves the development of the story with, normally, one shot seamlessly linked to the next so that the 'joins' do not draw attention to themselves ('continuity editing'). There will be relatively few sudden 'jumps' which, somewhat disconcertingly, make it feel as if a bit of film is missing. The sound is usually exploited in ways that complement rather than contradict what is being seen. Care is taken so that words can be heard even at the height of a raging storm or in the midst of the cacophony of battle. Special effects are the most obvious 'artificial' element yet here too it is normal practice for their use to serve the story, even allowing for a certain 'wow' factor to amaze and thrill audiences.

## In scene

Different locations evoke different ideas and moods. There is the harsh, dark cold world of barbarian Germany at the start of the film. There was originally a German fort in the script but presumably this would have detracted from the image of savage barbarians storming out of the forest. The opening landscape contrasts strongly with the image of a rich, peaceful, sun-kissed farm described by Maximus (an idyllic dream soon to be shattered). It, in turn, stands in stark contrast to the charred remains of his homestead after the attack by Commodus' men.

Next come the hot deserts where Proximo's training camp is located. It has all the isolation, indeed desolation, which reflects the plight of Maximus at that point in the story. Proximo's gladiator school was constructed on a hill next to a small town in Morocco, home to one of the oldest Casbahs in the world. Its streets helped to give the film a more authentic feel than otherwise might have been the case with totally artificial sets.

The magnificent cityscape of Rome itself is a third major setting, against whose splendour both politicians and masses seem petty. The way that it is brought so vividly to life also serves to add to the 'wow' factor, central to the

film's appeal. Again, the realistic feel of the film is partly augmented by the use, where possible of old buildings (or, rather, ruins) rather than specially constructed sets or purely digital creations.

## Dress code

*Gladiator* uses costume in a variety of ways. The most obvious is to distinguish different groups, Romans and barbarians, officers and soldiers, Roman patricians and 'plebs', masters and slaves and of course the gladiators themselves. Equally evident is the way costume is used to pick out individuals and underline personal characteristics. Thus the different gladiators are dressed quite distinctively.

It followed that the costumes of the Emperor's family would be the most elaborate. Lucilla, for example, comes clothed in luxurious fabrics like silk, satin, cashmere and chiffon, with gold threads and jewels, all signifying her status. By contrast the (unnamed) wife of Maximus is, very briefly, shown in much simpler, though still elegant, clothes. But there are also other considerations, especially the need to make armour light and malleable enough that would allow the actors to actually act.

Clarke (2002) draws attention to the way in which Commodus is shown wearing marble-like armour, evoking the marble busts of former emperors and thereby perhaps reminding audiences of his burning ambition. By contrast, Maximus is a simple man of honour and his clothing is comparatively plain, both at his height as a general and during his time as a gladiator.

A wide variety of props suggest both time periods (Rome at its height), characters, ideas and specific situations. Part and parcel of ancient warfare, for example, are catapults, swords, javelins and so forth. The power and wealth of Roman's ruling elite is suggested by fine goblets and many other items. Maximus' longing for his home and family is evoked by the little model figures he carries with him.

Props can also keep audiences interested. Repeated gladiatorial encounters can begin to pale, even when the combatants come clothed in all sorts of exotic gear and armed with striking weaponry such as tridents. Audience interest is recharged by use of props like chariots (and especially pile-ups).

Even something like soil can function as a prop. In this case it signifies the 'earthy' nature of Maximus. The plot emphasises that he is a 'simple' man living with his beloved family on their farm. His habit of rubbing his hands in the soil serves as a reminder of this. It is also a gesture that the 'refined' Commodus would never make, thus emphasising the gulf between protagonist and antagonist. Appropriately enough, one of the last actions of the film is that of Juba burying in the soil the family figurines that Maximus carried with him.

Even more gripping is the sudden appearance of roaring tigers. The creatures that Maximus has to confront in the arena are not digital creatures but flesh and blood members of the species raised in captivity. Indeed there are lions, zebras, oxen and an elephant in the film, all helping to give its visual interest and a 'natural' feel (i.e. as if they really would have been there).

The way audiences see such things can be strongly influenced by the differing kinds of lighting. The same is true in the theatre, though outdoor scenes in film-making also employ supplementary lights in many shots. The time of day (or year) when a scene is shot will also add its own qualities. A striking use of lighting in *Gladiator* is the contrast between two 'Romes'. One Rome is that of very bright, sometimes almost blinding scenes in the arena (underlining the fact that it is a moment when Maximus is 'on the spot', faced with the stark choice of 'do-or-die'). The other is full of shadows and dark corners, a world of plots and betrayals, one where individual heroism counts for less than clever subterfuge. Darkest of all is the penultimate scene in the dungeons below

**NOTES:**

# Film Language in *Gladiator*

the arena when Commodus deliberately cripples Maximus before the final fight.

Lighting (natural and/or artificial) is used within specific scenes. Various forms — key (main), fill and back lighting — may be used to suggest mood, underline a particular element within a scene, direct the audience's attention or even withhold information by placing a character or object in the shadows. Darkness can also suggest something suspicious or malevolent about a character. Not surprisingly Commodus is often shown in half-light or in the shadows. By contrast, the moment when Maximus dons his helmet and is 'reborn' as an invincible gladiator is brightly illuminated with a beam of light.

## Composition

Both the theatrical stage and the cinema screen have boundaries which 'frame' the action. What is left out of that frame may be as significant as what is within those edges. Inside the frame some things may be to the fore, others to the back. They may be placed at the centre, to the left or right in relation to each other. There will also be differences in the amount of space that certain things occupy within the total frame. Lines, shapes and patterns might be created by objects inside the frame, further enriching the overall composition. In film, then it is important to decode what the 'composition' of any given shot might communicate.

A typical example of the use of framing is to make the lead character 'stand out', dominating all other individuals and objects in the shot. Often Maximus dominates the frame as befits an action hero and leader of men, for example. By contrast, Commodus seems to steal into view as it were and often hovers around, reflecting his increasingly evil intent. At one point he almost pops into the frame from beneath a blanket of shields.

Alternatively, absences from a scene can be significant. Thus the initial absence of

Maximus from the post-opening battle celebrations underline the fact that he has only one thought — to return to his wife and son after years of absence. It further underlines the poignancy of subsequent events.

## In shot

Unique to film (and television) but impossible in the theatre is the way camerawork selects how the action is shown to viewers. That experience will be altered by choices in camera positioning (angles above or below and from the front, behind, left or right as well as distance from the action, ranging from extreme long shots to very tight close-ups) and in movement of the camera itself such as following a character.

Such choices might be used to give a certain point of view, perhaps letting the audience see what a character is seeing or, alternatively, see things of which the character is unaware. They can make a character seem subordinate to another or superior. Generally the film-maker, unlike the theatre director, has much greater power to make audiences concentrate on something they want to emphasise (e.g. the words coming out of a character by tight close-up on the mouth or a 'reaction shot' of a character's response to what he/she is hearing).

*Gladiator* illustrates what the film scholar Thomas Elsaesser has called 'engulfment' (quoted in Rushton, 2001). In the opening battle scene, so rapid is the cutting, so mobile the camera and so tight the close-ups that it is hard to know who is fighting whom. Instead we are buried in a torrent of images and sounds. We the audience may well be suitably astonished but we are none the wiser as to what precisely is going on (apart from the fact that there is a battle going on and that Maximus survives various threatening encounters).

Recreating the spectacle of ancient Rome

## Editing and special effects

After the actual shooting of a film comes the editing of all the footage taken. Extra sounds and optical effects are also added at this stage. Together they add further dimensions to the ways in which a film can communicate. Editing can, for example, make shots longer or shorter. The average shot length of *Gladiator* was 3.36 seconds, less than half the average of the more 'arty' *Spartacus* (King, 2002). The effect is to accentuate the feeling of excitement as one shot rapidly follows another. Though such choices may be felt to reflect the dominant practice in modern action-packed blockbusters, 'Soviet Montage' directors like Eisenstein, some 80 years ago, were cutting their films a lot faster than their American equivalents.

Editing can juxtapose characters, actions and scenes, intensifying the expressive force. The destruction of Maximus' family and farmstead is dramatised by first giving the viewer a panoramic view of his home. We see those about to be slaughtered in the middle of a rich pastoral idyll. But then we are suddenly shown the soldiers sent by Commodus charging towards the villa, intent on destruction.

In the same sequence, the film cross-cuts to Maximus riding home as fast as he can. Some readers may recall John Wayne desperately worrying about the fate of his kin back at the ranch in *The Searchers*. The sense of a

**NOTES:**

doomed race against time is built up by careful juxtaposition of shots from different places.

Choices about editing go together with initial camerawork and mise-en-scène. Thus the impact of the battle scene derives from various devices: constant switching of normal and high speed film, combined with jerky camera movements, rapid edits and, towards the end, employment of slow motion.

Understandably most attention was paid to the employment of digitally created imagery in *Gladiator*. But these are just one part of the armoury of movie special effects. Pyrotechnics play their fiery part. Some 16,000 actual flaming arrows plus several fireballs were launched in the opening battle scene, for example, though CGI enhanced the smoke trails.

Other effects are 'in-camera'. Some shots of the Colosseum seen on screen were created in this way, flopping over the negatives (having made sure that the actors are moving and carrying things on the correct side during the filming so that the illusion is not broken). Part of the Roman army was created by non-digital means, using Vistavision plates (a special 35mm film, with a widescreen effect, the results being a bit like a series of photographs). Devices like false limbs allowed individual fighters to be 'dismembered'.

It should be remembered that although computer-generated imagery can create things that otherwise would be either unacceptably dangerous or physically impossible, it can be a very costly technology. Older techniques sometimes retain a financial advantage.

## Sound world

Part of film language is what its audience hears. Sound has many qualities, all of which can simply complement what is being seen, forcefully underline the drama of a scene or, sometimes contradict the images on screen, perhaps for ironic effect. It may emanate from within what is being seen, e.g. the sound of a whip cracked on

screen (diegetic) or may be added from 'outside' the film as with most music (non-diegetic). They are often synchronised with the image though frequently there are sound 'bridges' when the sound of the following scene is heard a fraction before it is actually seen, thus alerting the audience to the change.

Film sound can be crudely broken into the human voice (monologues, conversation, crowd noises, etc.), music and various sound effects. All may be louder or softer, slower or faster, to the foreground or in the background. Their tonal quality may similarly change from the strident, martial tones of the brass section to romantic shimmering of the orchestral strings.

Human voices have other qualities such as dialect and accent. Actors might deliberately pause, stutter, mispronounce words and in many other ways communicate their thoughts and feelings. The rest of nature provides a veritable encyclopaedia of sounds, from the crack of thunder (used in the film when Maximus is taken prisoner by Quintus to suggest evil events ahead) to the happy chirp of a bird. Synthesisers and other audio equipment stretch the resources available to film-makers to seemingly endless possibilities. It might be worth stressing, then, that silence too can be an extremely powerful 'sound effect'.

The score of *Gladiator* was composed by Hans Zimmer with vocal inputs from Lisa Gerrard and additional material from Klaus Bedelt. Gerrard added the vocals that give the film, not least during the opening credits, its delicate and other-worldly quality, in sharp contrast to the scenes of violent action that punctuate the film. The pulsating excitement of those moments owe a great deal to the hard-edged chords that match the rhythm of fighters trading sword blows. Overall, the music underlines the contrast between the 'human' Maximus as would-be man of peace, longing to return to his family (underpinned by music with titles like 'Sorrow', 'Elysium' and 'Now We Are Free', for example),

and the heroic Maximus, general-turned-gladiator living in a world of brutal violence.

The music is itself scarcely 'Roman' (though it is hard to be sure precisely what that might be). The instruments used include Chinese and Armenian ones as well as synthesised sounds. A quite modern rock aesthetic pervades much of the score while at other points the influence of nineteenth century German composer Richard Wagner (especially regarding musical motifs to suggest the power and grandeur of Rome) and the British early twentieth century composer Gustav Holst (especially in the opening battle). But all that really matters is the effect — from the evocation of emotional tenderness to the fury of war and the mighty grandeur of Rome.

## Reading *Gladiator* – The opening sequence

Maximus, leader of men

Scott was careful to give his audience a big action scene early in the film, the absence of which had contributed to the unpopularity of the Antony Mann's film ***The Fall of the Roman Empire***. This analysis focuses on that opening sequence.

*Gladiator* is set when the Roman Empire at the height of its power. The opening action takes place in Germania, on the northern edge of the empire's borders, in AD 180. The film uses a normal device for communicating such

**NOTES:**

# Film Language in *Gladiator*

details: text on screen. After an opening prologue, viewers are plunged into a ferocious battle in which the Roman army, under the leadership of the main character, Maximus, defeats the barbarian hordes. Viewers are encouraged to identify with Maximus and his men. They are clearly the forces of civilisation while the barbarians are put in the role of those of ignorance and vicious savagery.

## Mise-en-scène

The scene is shot on location, not in a studio. The opening scene shows a man walking through a cornfield[1]. We see him gently touching the wheatears. The predominant colour here is a rich gold, perhaps suggesting happiness, prosperity or even contentment. However, it soon changes to steely greys, dark blues, browns and dark greens, matching the subsequent change of mood to one of conflict and violence.

The rest of the scene is set in a forestry plantation. Obviously such woodland did not exist at the time when the film is set, but it suggests the wild forests of Germany in which the Roman army has a tough fight on its hand against an enemy lurking in the woods. It is a mud-covered landscape dotted in the middle with charred stumps, suggesting that there has already been bitter fighting. The clothing of the men we see suggests that they are Roman soldiers. They are not wearing clean uniforms but look as if they have been on campaign for some time. The barbarians are dressed in animal furs and swarm around like a violent mob in contrast to the disciplined Romans.

One significant motif in the opening stages of the film is a bird taking flight. This is a popular device in movies to suggest freedom or perhaps the desire for it — in contrast to the restraints of duty or even repression and imprisonment. Part of the props in a battle scene is obviously weaponry. We see and hear Roman war engines hurling javelins and fire bombs at the barbarians.

The first man we see in the battle scene is an individual soldier. He has an intense expression on his face, perhaps contemplating things of great importance[2]. This suggests that he is in command since he is alone, whereas all the others are in rows. He is then seen purposefully striding through the ranks of his men. Their responses suggest that he is well respected leader.

Later he is positioned a bit higher than another officer with whom he has a conversation, making the latter look like his subordinate. The actor is Russell Crowe. He has the necessary rugged looks of an action film hero. Crowe physically dominates much of this sequence, underlining his heroic stature. He combines a sense of physical strength and mental toughness with a certain gentleness and even serenity.

Before the battle starts, another Roman is picked out by the editing. Most viewers will deduce that he is a more senior figure, perhaps the Emperor himself. The opening legend mentioned the 'rule of the Caesars' so the connection is not hard to make. His decisions about the future of his empire will drive the narrative of the film so it is important that viewers are made aware of his presence early in the film. His deeply etched face and white hair suggest age, experience, leadership and perhaps a certain tiredness with life.

## Framing, shot composition and camerawork

After the opening prologue, there is an establishing shot of the battlefield which enables the viewer to see where the Roman army is located as well as the woods from which the barbarians will emerge[3]. It is shot from a camera craning up to reveal the whole scene. From this master shot the rest of the action develops in detail. We see the horse bringing back the body of a dead messenger then the first barbarians from the point of view of the Romans. Most shots are from their perspective and often that of the hero, Maximus.

The esteem in which Maximus is held by his men is communicated via tracking shots which show him striding through their ranks from which the soldiers return respectful acknowledgement[4] (this composition is repeated with Maximus among admiring fellow gladiators later in the African arena). This lends more energy to the shot than would a more static frame. Other shots show weapons of war being prepared, again fuelling the viewer's expectations. Closer shots make the audience concentrate on an exchange between Maximus and his deputy Quintus.

The dialogue poses the question of whether the barbarians will fight. We see their 'answer' visually as a long shot from the point of view of the Roman army shows a horse bearing a headless rider appearing from the forest[5]. It is the Roman negotiator who has been beheaded by the barbarians. They then appear and a medium close-up of a huge barbarian shows him holding the severed head. This underlines the savagery of the enemy that the Romans face.

There is a cut back to Maximus giving the orders to prepare for battle. He commands: 'unleash hell'. The sense of anticipation reaches new heights. A cut to a close-up focuses on his dog being unleashed, not just a visual play on his words but, perhaps, also an allusion to Shakespeare's line, 'let slip the dogs of war' in his play *Julius Caesar*.

During the ensuing battle, the cameras are often placed in the heart of the action, plunging the viewer into the maelstrom. We see the battle from a variety of shots. Long shots allow us to see the geography of the fight — the position and movements of the rival armies[6]. Medium shots give us more details as, for example, barbarians are drenched in burning liquid or impaled by the javelins. Close-ups underline the sheer intensity of combat, including shots of wild eyes,

1

2

3

screaming mouths and swinging sword arms. The use of an unsteady, handheld camera and a sudden loss of focus build this sensation.

Tracking shots are also used to give the sensation of charging along with the Roman cavalry as they encircle the barbarians from the rear. Close-ups also show the dog loyally racing after its master, a common sentimental device in action movies. The grainy look of the film also gives an extra sense of realism, like a rough-and-ready *vérité* documentary actually filmed under fire. A pair of close-ups brings the sequence to an end. One is Maximus proclaiming victory, the other the Emperor sighing in relief, 'Thank God'. The sunlight lights up the Emperor's white hair giving him more status. This sums up what has transpired and slows down what has been an adrenalin-pumping pace.

## Sound

There is not a great deal of dialogue in what, after all, is a battle scene. Perhaps the most important is the exchange between Maximus and his deputy Quintus. We can hear a slight note of resentment and perhaps jealousy on the part of Quintus as Maximus overrules his objections to the battle plan. After the appearance of the Germanic tribesmen, the sound is dominated by their savage chanting, building the audience's anticipation of a bloody confrontation.

Music and sound effects are particularly important. The prologue has calm but mysterious music, with wind and sting instruments, then a female voice, to the fore. It has echoes of the rather mystical 'Celtic' music heard in other modern movies such as *Braveheart* and *Titanic*. It sets up themes associated with the hero and his tragic destiny as well as contrasts the sounds of battle soon to burst out. In the prologue we also hear happy children's voices, reinforcing the pastoral imagery and its connotations of peace and serenity, soon to be broken by the sound of war.

After the opening section and as the action gets underway, we hear music with a very martial air, not unlike the theme of Mars (i.e. 'Roman God of War') from Holst's Planet Suite. We also hear the whooshing sound of the catapult bolts and fireballs flying through the air before crashing to the ground. However, some of the music, especially the slow-motion sequence at the end of the battle, is tinged with sadness, like the famous death scene of Sergeant Elias in *Platoon* (1986). It replaces the sound of metal upon metal sword and human screams which are heard during the earlier part of the battle.

## Sound and vision editing

After the opening credits, a fade to black takes the viewer to a close-up slow-motion shot of a man's left hand as he walks through a cornfield. We see him gently touching the wheatears. The shot does not give us any hard information and audience anticipation is likely to increase as a result since most viewers will want to know the man's identity and the significance of his actions. We soon find out who he is but the meaning of the field is not made fully clear.

After the opening sequence, the editing becomes progressively more rapid to keep up the tension as the film cuts from one shot to another. The editing also keeps viewers focused on the hero Maximus and his particular experience of the battle. He is shown to be a tough fighter, no armchair general, a portent of his skills as a gladiator.

Shots of another key figure, the Emperor, are edited into the pre-battle sequence, to make viewers aware that he is watching the ensuing fight and to underline that this is the climactic battle of the campaign. The fact that he is there also sets up a contrast with his weak son who arrives late, after the fighting is over.

During the battle, individual barbarians are also picked out in medium and close shots, especially a mountain of a man who kills several Romans before being felled himself. This helps to maintain a human scale to the drama. Later in the battle, there is a switch to slow motion. This helps to spotlight the brutality of the fighting but perhaps also suggests the tragedy of war since the accompanying music at this point is slow and sombre. Another edit picks out Maximus as he backs into one of his men and turns to kill him before recognising that he is a comrade, showing the chaos of the action. The end of the battle is marked by an edit which sees Maximum proclaiming victory.

The film not only uses sound and moving images: the opening credits start with text on the screen. The word 'Gladiator' appears by itself, in a black, hard Roman typeface, rather statue-like, against a background of swirling sepia-tinged smoke, perhaps suggesting the mists of time. A short sequence of text on screen quickly informs the audience where and when the action is taking place. It stresses that what viewers are about to see is not just any battle but the climax of the Emperor's campaign.

4

5

6

# Narrative in *Gladiator*

The hero and his helpers

'A hero will rise' (*Gladiator* **poster tagline)**

**The construction of the *Gladiator* story follows the conventions established by older historical epics but with a few twists that owe more to contemporary movie-making. Ridley Scott himself described *Gladiator* as 'a great, old-fashioned yarn', though he also stressed that he had brought 'new' life to a story already tackled in** *The Fall of the Roman Empire.*

Most stories, be it telling a joke, recounting a holiday or providing a witness statement, usually require certain information about who, what, when, where, how and, of course, why. Films — fictional and documentary — are no different. Otherwise their audience could not sense what is going on. There are many different ways this information could be imparted.

The concept of narrative relates the techniques through which these details are communicated; in other words, how a story is told rather than the actual story itself.

That of ***Gladiator*** might, for example, have

been told through the eyes of Juba. It could have opened with his first encounter with Maximus, followed by a flashback in which Juba explains how he ended up a gladiator. Alternatively, the story might have been delivered by Quintus, perhaps as an old man ruefully looking back on how he mistakenly betrayed Maximus. The actual story itself would have remained the same but the way it was told would have been quite different.

There seem to be recurrent features in human storytelling. Certain common features seem to link stories and storytelling from ancient myths, legends, fairy stories and folk tales to contemporary TV soap operas and broadcast news. Of course, there are variations and exceptions, making it possible to distinguish mainstream narrative systems from experimental non-mainstream ones.

None the less, there are certain elements that all share, whether treated conventionally or otherwise. Essentially there is a sequence of events happening in some space, spread over a period of time. Central features of the way this

succession of happenings is related are:

**Narration and points of view** (who is the narrator and through whose eyes in particular, if any, are the events experienced).

**Settings** (the where and when).

**Chronology** (length and sequencing) and physical space (placing of action and movement from one place to another).

**Causation** (what makes things happen) and, in mainstream narratives, connections between the events that unfold.

**Characters and their motivations**, often including some personally set goal or externally given mission).

**Major and minor 'players' in the action**, the functions they perform in the overall story, as well as the ways in which audiences are encouraged to react to them (identification, sympathy, indifference, hostility, etc.).

**Story structure**: beginning, subsequent developments and final resolution (often with an opening state of normality or equilibrium followed by some sort of disruption and attempts to restore some sort of new balance or order).

**Plots and sub-plots.** Many stories, especially ones involving some sort of detection, involve 'red herrings' and other false trails (e.g. characters misreading information or misinterpreting someone's intentions). Very common are sub-plots, possibly to add variety and interest, though in film the need to offer points of appeal to a wider audience is often the dominant reason rather than the 'needs' of the story itself.

The above narrative choices create a world, a diegesis, which viewers/listeners/readers enter. In conventional narratives, it is a believable world or, more precisely, a plausible one. Most

**NOTES:**

viewers of **Gladiator** will make a 'negotiated' reading of the film's story. They probably will think that it is a bit unlikely that Maximus could have got his revenge but will go along with the film since it does not stretch the boundaries of plausibility to breaking point (which an unconventional film might deliberately do).

The idea of a single but determined hero standing up to be counted in the face of seemingly impossible odds reaches back into the realms of myth and legend. Indeed it pervades many areas of life. Thus, both football and other sports competitions as well as other contests such as political elections are often reported in terms of David versus Goliath (with an assumption that most people favour the 'little guy' against the big battalions). Maximus' loyalty to the dead Emperor turns him into an outcast. Thus, he becomes the 'underdog' but duly bites back and overcomes his powerful enemy. That he dies at the moment of victory similarly draws upon ancient storytelling traditions.

Humankind also seems to want explanations and meanings. The ancients might have seen various phenomena as signs that the Gods were angry. Thus, names were put on certain stars as if they actually had significant patterns beyond mere randomness. Today we use broad concepts like 'globalisation', 'axis of evil' or 'global warming', but all are attempts to make sense of life and put things into some sort of meaningful order.

## Narratology

A number of cultural theorists have studied the core stories that humans concoct and the way they tell them ('narratology'). In ancient Greece, Aristotle in particular spotlighted the difference between story and storytelling. Vladimir Propp (1895-1970), a modern cultural theorist, studied the common elements from which his native Russian folk tales were fashioned.

Several of Propp's character archetypes are present in **Gladiator**. Apart from obvious ones like hero and villain, there is Lucilla, Propp's heroine (of sorts), Marcus Aurelius ('father' figure who gives the hero a task, in this case that of saving Rome, with an attendant reward, the imperial throne) and Promixo, Propp's 'mentor' (trainer) and perhaps also 'donor' since he gives the hero a special talisman or clue ('win the crowd') plus various other helpers and blockers.

As suggested by Propp the hero of **Gladiator** is given a mission but the actions of Commodus change it into the more personal one of vengeance. Yet its accomplishment will at the same time lead to the achievement of the original goal, Rome's salvation from its evil Emperor. Of course, contrary to Propp's model, the hero does not win the princess nor get the throne — he dies — but he does get a kind of reward, being reunited with his family in Elysium.

Tzvetan Todorov (1939) spotlighted in particular the pattern of an initial equilibrium then disruption, recognition of and reaction to that disturbance, attempts to resolve it, followed finally by new equilibrium. In **Gladiator**, Maximus certainly personifies Todorov's notion of 'transformation' in which his circumstances and prospects are well and truly turned upside down by the disturbances unleashed by Commodus' murderous actions. **Gladiator** might not quite possess the structural circularity suggested by Todorov — the hero does die — but in other respects equilibrium is restored after further disturbances (triggered largely by the growing instability of Commodus).

Another cultural theorist, Algirdas Greimas, drew attention to core ingredients such as the tasks and struggles that face a story's characters. Thus, Maximus has to escape his would-be executioners. He must then survive the journey to Africa as well as triumph in the gladiatorial ring as he encounters increasingly dangerous situations, until finally the climactic struggle

with his enemy.

Greimas also spotlighted another fundamental convention: the establishment or breaking of contracts (in the broad sense). So Maximus has a sort of contract with Marcus Aurelius as does Commodus by virtue of kinship but the latter violently breaks it. Maximus refuses the new 'contract' offered by Commodus but later establishes new ones with his helpers in Rome. Greimas also highlighted the narrative role of departures and arrivals. The major 'acts' of **Gladiator** discussed below end with a departure (end of Act 1 from Germania, end of Act 2 from Africa) and start with an arrival (first, the appearance of the barbarian army, its second scene being initiated by the arrival of Commodus; second, Maximus arriving in Africa; and third, gladiators arriving in Rome).

Claude Lévi-Strauss looked at the deep beliefs that underlie human culture. He called them 'myths' in the sense of universal truths. They are taken for granted, seemingly natural rather than specially created (and, as such, questionable or replaceable). Thus, we tend to see things in binary terms (e.g. on/off, light/dark, food/non-food, friend/enemy). **Gladiator** certainly illustrates that pattern with that most commonplace of oppositions, hero/villain (with attendant binary evaluations of good/bad). It is not the only one, however, others including Roman/barbarian, ageing father/young son, loyal servant/treacherous lieutenant and senator/Emperor. It is the tensions between such opposing forces that drive a story.

The above stress on repeated features should not be allowed to minimise the sheer diversity of narrative structures and devices as well as the variations in mood, characterisation and other features that have created such a rich treasure trove of stories, not least storytelling movies. Perhaps a comparison might be made with architecture. There are some elements common to most buildings but they do come in an amazing range of shapes and sizes.

**NOTES:**

# Narrative in *Gladiator*

## Story and plot

Sometimes a distinction is made between story and plot. Strictly speaking the latter is what we see and hear in *Gladiator*. But there is clearly much more going on. We infer, for example, that there has been a long brutal war in Germania before the opening battle of the plot. We assume that Commodus organised a raiding party to destroy the home of the now rebel Maximus but we do not actually see the murders and despoilation, only their aftermath. Most viewers probably would take for granted that the worst evils of the reign of Commodus cease after his death and that Juba, last seen heading home, safely arrives there. That total world, explicit and implicit, is the story.

The film generally follows a straight chronological order. There are no flashbacks though as suggested below there is a hint of flashforward to the heavenly lands of Elysium at the very opening scene. Both plot and story of *Gladiator* last a great deal longer than the film itself. There is also enormous time compression at many points of the film. The aftermath of the battle (picking up the wounded, etc.) would have lasted far longer than what is shown on screen.

The film uses a 'third person' narration. We the audience are 'all knowing' (insofar as the director and his crew present us with information). We watch the events unfold as if the characters were in some gigantic goldfish bowl. We may surmise what characters are thinking but no use is made of 'first person' devices like a voice-over. The characters themselves only know what they see and hear within the narrative world of the film (sometimes called diegesis). By contrast, we, the audience, are privy to much more information, derived from scenes from which certain characters are absent, or from sights and sounds when characters are present but their positioning prevents them from seeing or hearing.

## Narrative construction

*Gladiator* has a clear storyline, where one thing seems to lead logically to the next with obvious motives and in a general linear progression, some minor diversions apart, towards a climactic ending. Indeed, it is so straightforward that possible complications like sub-plots are shunned (unless one counts hints of on-going feelings of love between Maximus and Lucilla and even then such affection still serves the core plot of revenge).

There is an equally well defined setting for the story. It is made clear at the very start via text on the screen, explaining not just the historical period and location but also the particular events about to unfold on screen. The three major locations almost function as acts in a play. Act 1, which might be called 'Downfall of a Hero' is set in Germania. Act 2, 'Trials and Tribulations', takes place at the gladiator training school in North Africa while the concluding Act, 'A Hero's Revenge', unfolds in Rome.

There is a straightforward structure here. At the beginning, there is comparative equilibrium. A successful general is waging one more battle. But then disruption follows. The Emperor is killed and his murderer usurps the throne. Maximus' refusal to swear loyalty is the trigger for the subsequent developments: first his flight, then the slaying of his family and finally his search for vengeance. Within these sequences there are minor plot points on which events turn. Critical is Maximus' decision to fight as a gladiator.

'Act 3' takes the plot to its climax. It does include another narrative device, the 'complication'. In this case, Commodus discovers that the previously anonymous 'Spaniard' is in fact his sworn enemy, Maximus, who is thereby put in greater danger. As with most conventional narratives, there is darkness before the dawn. The plan to rally the army against Commodus is foiled while, when

prisoner again, Maximus is deliberately incapacitated, stacking the odds in Commodus' favour. The climax comes with the death of both protagonist and antagonist.

But there is also a 'denouement' in which all loose strings are neatly tied up (the dialogue establishes what will happen to characters like Gracchus and we see Juba going home a free man). Things are back to some sort of equilibrium. Wrongs have been righted and it seems peace will prevail. As such, there is closure. There can be no Maximus Part 2, though there are openings for further plotlines, notably the young Lucius (at the time of writing, *Gladiator 2* was still a possibility).

*Gladiator* has no *deus ex machina*, something of the blue that resolves the problem. It might strike some as far-fetched that Maximus, despite being wounded, still overcomes Commodus. None the less, like the rest of the film, it is plausible within the terms set by the narrative. Also and unlike several contemporary action movies, there is no false ending where action suddenly starts up again (e.g. *The Terminator*'s killer robot suddenly coming back to 'life'). Instead there is a comparatively clear-cut ending.

These events are character-driven. They do not happen because of an earthquake, forest fire, plague or some other natural event. Nor do they result from human, but none the less external, causes such as war, economic crisis or broad social phenomena like racism and poverty. Supernatural forces and extra-terrestrial interventions play no part.

It is the perception of Marcus Aurelius that his son is unsuitable to be ruler that leads him to offer the throne to Maximus. It is jealousy, twisted ambitions and violent instability that make Commodus murder his father on hearing this news. It is Maximus' sense of honour that makes him reject the hand of friendship offered by Commodus. It is Proximo's memories of his own youth that make him help Maximus. It is

**NOTES:**

her feelings of affection that make Lucilla help Maximus against her own brother. And, of course, it is a burning desire for vengeance that makes Maximus seek out Commodus.

The personal and the political are structurally blended in the narrative through two parallel and interacting tales. There is the individual crisis of Maximus which is inseparably linked to the crisis of succession to the Imperial Throne. Maximus' personal struggle in the aftermath of his arrest, near execution and enslavement, in the background of which lie the ruins of his family life, parallels the power struggle in Rome, behind which are the loss of decency and justice in the body politic. Maximus' attainment of his personal goal, revenge, is at the same time resolution of the political crisis since the evil upstart, Commodus, is now dead and power has returned to the (good) hands of Gracchus and his associates.

## Characters

Most narratives are based on individual characters. This may seem blindingly obvious. Yet there are films without discrete individuals, such as Godfrey Reggio's *Koyaanisqatsi* (1983), a string of striking images minus any personal dimension. In many 'Soviet Montage' films like the famous *Battleship Potemkin*, the audience barely gets to know the names of the people they are seeing, let along anything about their personalities or background.

This is not the dominant tradition, however. Identifiable and understandable characters are central to its narrative structures. This practice is not just the rule in fictional films. News reports and documentaries too are usually constructed around a few individuals, whose experiences are used to shed light on the wider situation.

Conventional narratives normally have a binary structure, setting two individuals (or groups, as in cops versus robbers or cowboys/cavalry versus Indians) against each other, protagonists

and antagonists. The protagonist of *Gladiator* is Maximus and the audience sees the event of the story largely through his eyes. He is given a number of defining characteristics such as physical prowess, courage, tenacity, loyalty, decency and integrity. In short, he is the embodiment of the Roman army motto, 'Strength and Honour'.

In some ways, he is a figure cut from traditional hero narratives. This is not just in the sense that he is brave and steadfast, like William Wallace in *Braveheart*, Spartacus or Robin Hood. More significantly, like those other heroes, he is the victim of events that conspire to force him into the role of wronged man, thirsting for revenge.

Yet, at the same time, he is a rather reluctant hero, initially not tempted by the mission given him by Marcus Aurelius. Comparisons might be made with modern action film characters like Officer John McClane, who, in the *Die Hard* series, keeps finding himself in deep and unwanted trouble. There is also a degree of bitterness and disillusionment in Maximus, unlike Robin Hood who merrily kept his faith in good King Richard. He is also scornful of the crowds whereas Robin was perfectly willing to acknowledge the cheering peasants and townsfolk. Maximus is more an extension of the moodier Ben-Hur.

Like Captain Miller in *Saving Private Ryan*, Maximus yearns to return to what, in his words, would appear to be a life of domestic bliss. Unlike Miller, his dream is shattered early in the movie when Commodus orders the slaughter of his wife and eight-year-old son after Maximus refuses to pledge loyalty. Maximus is thereby left with nothing but a burning desire for revenge to fuel his fight for survival in the gladiatorial arena to which fate delivers him.

The challenge facing the film's protagonist is intensified in another way. At various points it is made clear by the dialogue that he is an

outsider. Even at the height of his power, he was not part of Roman's inner circles (note his somewhat uncomfortable behaviour at the post-battle feast). His 'otherness' is further underlined by his being called 'the Spaniard' while a gladiator, before his true identity is revealed.

His refusal to compromise at key moments deepens his predicament. The narrative provides the specific motivation for this: sense of honour. His essential decency is underlined at various points too, not least in the way he kills only to survive, not for pleasure (thus he is shown sparing the life of the gladiator Tigris of Gaul).

His antagonist is Commodus. In narrative terms, such a character usually comes in two forms, either a larger-than-life monster, devoid of any attractive features or someone who invites a certain sympathy or at least understanding. Commodus is clearly the latter. He is portrayed as a man emotionally crippled by a neglectful father, as is made clear in the post-battle feast scene. On his way there, he is shown almost clinging for security to his sister Lucilla. To further cast Commodus in a bad light, his father Marcus Aurelius is turned into a somewhat saintly figure, an impression underlined by his white hair and world-weary expression.

These choices in the characterisation of Commodus create more scope for his subsequent development during the course of the story, with Commodus becoming progressively more deranged, as opposed to someone who, from the start, is totally mad. Like Maximus, Commodus too is well defined — jealous, arrogant, cruel, self-pitying, though he is no craven coward. He too is given motivations. Classical narrative tradition demands that he be a dangerous and, in that sense, worthy adversary.

*Gladiator* somewhat toys with another narrative structuring device. It is quite common to create protagonists and antagonists who are mirror images of each other. Thus, Ethan Edwards (John Wayne) shares certain

**NOTES:**

qualities with the Indian chief Scar in *The Searchers*. In *Heat* (1995), the cop (Al Pacino) leads a life not unlike that of the thief (Robert De Niro).

However, it is more common for movies first to suggest similarities but then make clear the differences. Thus, in **Lord of the Rings**, Gandalf and Saruman are like each other in many ways but the narrative partly rests on the premise that they will choose separate roads. Commodus does say to Maximus that 'we are not so different, you and I'. But Maximus is not someone to be tempted by the Dark Side and the plot runs its conventional course.

## Helpers and others

In line with most narrative structures, there is a set of secondary characters. The character of Lucilla is at first sight something of a spoilt brat, living a life of luxury and used to getting her ways. Yet it is also made clear that there was some sort of bond with Maximus in the past. According to actress Connie Nielsen, the script indicated that Lucilla had 'some sense of principles'. This enables her to function as a helper, aiding the hero in his mission.

Her son has a different role. His admiration for Maximus functions in a way as a surrogate for those sat in the audience, equally admiring the hero's endeavours. Within the story itself, he is also a point of vulnerability on 'Team Maximus'. Through him, Lucilla's commitment to help Maximus can be tested as Commodus makes menacing threats to Lucilla about both her own future and that of her son. The boy also functions as a reminder of Maximus' lost son. Their exchanges further spotlight how Maximus is still a good man: he has not lost all decency in a self-destructive vendetta.

Juba helps Maximus directly when Maximus is captured by the slave traders. But the character also functions as a moral compass insofar as he still has a family and has not lost sight of the need to look beyond revenge. Help can come in other ways. Marcus Aurelius is like a father figure, a role

taken over by Proximo (he really ought to be called Proximus), who continues the supply of good advice to aid Maximus on his way. Maximus' former servant later acts as a helpful messenger.

But Commodus too has his helpers. Quintus betrays Maximus against whom he is shown to feel certain resentments, pledging his support to the new Emperor and ordering the arrest of his former general. However, there is a process of character development here too. In the climactic fight between Maximus and Commodus in the arena, Quintus changes sides again, thereby facilitating the final act of revenge. Without this deed, Maximus could not have accomplished his mission and the film could not have come to the conclusion to which events have been inexorably leading.

## Analysing narrative

The following analysis focuses on the beginning of the film. The opening sequence serves to introduce the film's hero the Roman general Maximus. An opening prologue, with what we learn later to be the general walking through a field of wheat, shows a character of some sensitivity and thoughtfulness. This short scene creates something of an enigma. It is not clear who he is, where he is or why he is there. The answer is kept back until the final denouement at the end of the film. This scene might even to be said to be a flashforward insofar as it anticipates what is to come.

The next scene, visually a strong contrast to the one before it, spotlights that Maximus is also a man of action, a strong, determined figure, a true leader of men, venerated by his troops. By the end of the extract, his character is fully established. It is clear that he is the main character of the story. The sequence also establishes the narrative themes of strength, honour, freedom and loyalty which run through the rest of the story.

The Roman army is about to face the barbarian hordes. Their brutal nature is

underlined when a Roman envoy is sent back dead, his headless body strapped to his horse. The Roman army readies itself with Maximus quickly taking control of the situation. Though his main subordinate, Quintus, questions some of his decisions, Maximus decisively spells out the plan for battle. These disagreements also set the scene for the betrayal of Maximus by Quintus. At the same time, audience expectations of the spectacle to come are being built up.

The subsequent battle sequence delivers the spectacle associated with the grandest of epics. The length of the fight is somewhat compressed in terms of time but tries to convince in terms of realism. The audience is involved in the fight in that Scott has encouraged viewers to identify with Maximus and his part in the battle is the core of the narrative at this point in the film. The action seems very plausible. At one point, Maximus backs into one of his men and turns to kill him before recognising that he is a comrade.

The sequence is brought to a close by two significant punctuation marks. The first is Maximus proclaiming victory. He may have triumphed on the battlefield but his personal success soon proves short-lived. The second is his Emperor, Marcus Aurelius, sighing in relief that the fight is over. We are now introduced to another significant character. The Emperor is old and tired. The audience soon finds out that he fears for the future of Rome.

After the battle, the audience is also introduced to the Emperor's son, Commodus, and daughter, Lucilla. The weak but ruthless and cruel Commodus is to be the architect of Maximus' downfall but his sister, an old love of Maximus will help the hero gain his vengeance. The scene has been set for the main events of the story.

**NOTES:**

# Representations of Reality in *Gladiator*

Conflicted Lucilla, confused Commodus ©*Joel Finler Archive*

**'This is a pleasant fiction is it not?'** (Lucilla in *Gladiator*)

**Most movies are fictional products. They make few, if any, claims to be factually correct documentaries. Yet even the most far-fetched film says something about the real world. All movies contain values and messages. They may not be consciously created, deliberate attempts to encourage certain ideas and behaviours. They may not be understood nor accepted by their audiences. None the less, films both reflect and encourage certain ways of thinking and doing.**

It is the study of 'representation' that particularly seeks to reveal the picture painted of the world in films. It is easiest in the case of overtly political films like Michael Moore's polemic against the gun lobby, *Bowling for Columbine* (2002), 'crime-does-not-pay' morality tales or patriotic war movies. Yet, seemingly 'non-ideological' entertainment movies also deal with individuals, people of different social strata, gender, ethnicity and age, cultural sub-groups, organisations, cultures, places and events.

In doing so, they necessarily make statements about what is normal, acceptable, desirable, beautiful, fashionable, successful, praiseworthy, important or otherwise. They are particularly influential in such presentations when audiences have no direct experience of the subject matter against which they might compare what is being screened.

It should be stressed that what is not represented may be as potent as what is shown. Misrepresentation may involve the exaggeration of certain features at the expense of others or the use of excessively simplistic stereotypes. Such distortions need not necessarily be negative ones. Misrepresentation can discriminate in favour as well as against. Audience responses can range from enthusiastic acceptance to hostile rejection. Audiences are not blank slates on which movie-makers can write whatever they want. Instead people filter the ideas and feelings films communicate.

No viewer of *Gladiator* could have first-hand experience of what it depicts and very few would have done serious academic study of what is known about the realities of ancient Rome. Discussion of the picture the film paints of the world logically might start from its view of history. However, what it may be saying about contemporary society deserves even closer scrutiny.

## Representing history

'Someone (should) get Ridley Scott a history book' according to a note posted in the IMDb message board. The comment was made in reference to *Kingdom of Heaven* and its alleged distortion of the history of the Crusades. The same thought probably went through the minds of several critics of *Gladiator* too.

The film is riddled with historical inaccuracies. They range from distortions of the actual lives of real people like Commodus to errors regarding costume and other details. Commodus became Emperor in AD 180 as in *Gladiator* but reigned for 12 years, not the 3 years depicted in the film, surviving his sister, Lucilla. He did not die in the arena but was eventually strangled to death, on the orders of Roman senators frightened by his murderous megalomania.

Historians often stress that sex was an unusually prominent feature of Roman life as the surviving 'frisky' frescoes at Pompeii testify. Scott chose to omit this dimension. This may make the audience focus solely on the tragedy of Maximus but none the less, it misrepresents Roman realities. Similarly, there is little dirt and squalor in *Gladiator*'s Rome.

There is, of course, an obvious response, namely that *Gladiator* is a work of entertainment. It makes no claims to be some documentary about Roman history. Yet this defence is not entirely satisfactory. Film-makers, it could be argued, should bear some responsibility for an educational role that unavoidably falls on their shoulders. Historians

**NOTES:**

# Representations of Reality in *Gladiator*

like Allen Ward further chide the makers of *Gladiator* on the grounds that the real story of Commodus is even more exciting and interesting than the movie.

## Past and present

More important than factual accuracy per se is the question of why a film-maker might choose to show history in certain ways. A film like *Gladiator* is not just a film about history but also a film produced by history, i.e. something created by particular people at a particular juncture of time. As such they can tell us much about how people — both film-makers and film audiences — see things, both in their own times as well as times gone by.

*Gladiator*, then, is not just a representation, accurate or otherwise, of ancient Rome and the gladiatorial arena. It also makes statements about the here and now. It might do this deliberately or unintentionally. These messages might be accepted, rejected or not even noticed by its viewers but they are still there to be analysed.

Franzoni, the writer of *Gladiator*, is himself very clear about this. He says he 'wanted it to be about the twentieth century world. That's why we had a gladiator agent — God knows if those people really existed. Look, we were trying to get at a truth about Rome and about us. If forgoing literal accuracy is better for conveying the truth, I'll do that any day'.

He also saw it as a movie dealing in universal verities, not least that people have to kill simply to stay alive. *Gladiator* thus features what Franzoni calls 'eternal bravery and eternal cowardice'. The film's star Russell Crowe echoes such sentiments: 'This movie deals with important subjects such as political intrigue and religious persecution' (*USA Today*).

## Reality film

Discussion of representation in *Gladiator* raises a related issue, that of 'realism'. Of course, even the viewer most immersed in the spectacle of either film knows that the movies

are still a construction. Those people dying on screen are not really being killed. In fact, there are only a few moments of documentary footage and an equally small number of photographs that actually show people being killed in battle. So simulations are needed to depict combat as well as many other dangerous and otherwise hard-to-film aspects of reality.

The problem is that viewers often see some artifices as more real than others. Frequently films are praised (or condemned) by virtue of their apparent 'realism'. Even the 'realistic' *Saving Private Ryan* does not depict soldiers soiling their trousers nor does it show the long, long hours of sheer boredom that characterise the life of the average trooper.

*Gladiator* contains many quite unreal scenes. For example, in the opening battle scene, the Roman cavalry are depicted in an exciting charge through the woods. Amazingly, no horses crash into branches or tumble on undergrowth. One might also wonder what happens to Maximus' pet wolf which saves his life then mysteriously vanishes. The thrill of the spectacle will distract most viewers' minds from such anomalies.

There is a thriving cottage industry publishing books about continuity errors and other mistakes in movies. The important thing is appreciation that films are simply artifices. It is only that some feel more realistic than others. Otherwise all movies are no different to, say, paintings or plays. A film can be appreciated in and of itself, regardless of whether it is 'unrealistic'.

## Messages and values

The most complex part of any analysis of 'representation' in a film concerns deeper matters of beliefs — what a film suggests about how people could or should think about, value and do things. It can do this in a number of ways. The most obvious is when a movie takes a particular stand, for instance, the attack on miscarriages of justice and the machinations of the British 'Establishment' in Jim Sheridan's *In*

*the Name of the Father* (1993).

At times, such messages can be quite ambiguous as in the closing scene of Kubrick's *Full Metal Jacket* (1987) which could be interpreted as a critique of American involvement in the Vietnam War, an endorsement of it or simply a neutral picture of men in combat. To underline a point made earlier, viewers do not simply absorb what they are seeing and hearing but actively select and interpret in the light of their own interests, experiences and opinions.

Furthermore, a film's message may lie not in what it includes but rather what is left out. It can be these 'absences' that are significant. Similarly, the messages given out in a film do not have to be intentional on the part of its makers. They may well not be conscious of what is being said, especially when it comes to values and attitudes that are deeply ingrained in society and as such are taken as 'natural'.

Any analysis of a given film or film-maker might draw upon one or more schools of thought, each offering their own methodologies and frames of reference. Many focus on how an individual's view of reality is socially constructed by films, other media texts and society as a whole (i.e. individuals do not view the world simply through their own, 'virgin' eyes). Marxist theorists often link the ideas presented by the media to the interests of society's ruling class. Feminists, by contrast, spotlight what is being said about gender and ways in which men may be subordinating women (on and off the film screen). So-called 'postmodernist' theorists firmly focus on the film's audience. They argue that understanding a text like a film does not depend on its maker's intentions but on the subjective responses of its consumer.

## The world according to *Gladiator*

Though *Gladiator* would appear to be a straight story devoid of deeper values, certain

**NOTES:**

attitudes underpin its tale, albeit at the level of fairly simple homilies. Further, they are rather confused if not contradictory. There is a quite conservative strand to some of the ideas in the film, especially in its first half (Germania and Africa). Hardship and adversity are but part and parcel of life, burdens to be endured stoically in the manner of Maximus. Tribulations like warfare and political corruption are depicted as immutable features of the human condition. In one way, then, the film's value system might be seen as disempowering: there is no point in struggling to improve the world if it is inevitably full of grief and suffering.

However, this is an American movie and the dominant ideology in the USA (as in most parts of the industrialised world) is that of 'progress' and a corresponding 'can-do' attitude: things can and will get better. This worldview dominates the second half of the film once the plot reaches Rome. Certainly Maximus has to undergo severe trials yet he manages to turn the tables on his opponents. Of course, he dies in the end but the narrative makes clear that power will be returned to its rightful holders (and Maximus got, in a certain sense, what he wanted too).

At a number of points in the film, it is made clear that Commodus was ignoring urgent social problems in Rome so his subsequent demise opens the door to a better Rome. Indeed the faith in this political outcome is such that the script entertains the surely bizarre notion that had Maximus' original escape plan succeeded and the army under his leadership overthrown Commodus, power would simply have then been handed back by the military to the legal authorities (if only the real world were like that!).

## Class divide

So some things can be altered but not others. One thing in particular seems immutable: the notion of hierarchy. **Gladiator** depicts society as a two-tier social system. There are elite figures — emperors, senators, generals and

their relatives plus those who directly work for the ruling class, notably Quintus, Proximus and Cassius (the games organiser). Like those traditional schoolbooks that portrayed history as the story of Kings and Queens, of the rich and powerful few, **Gladiator** primarily deals in social elites.

Then there are the others, the masses. They only exist as a crowd. They die in battle, they throng the streets of Rome and they fill the Colosseum. They may boo, they may cheer, they may even influence whether a defeated gladiator is to be put to the sword but otherwise they are mere onlookers, incapable of collective action. They are not agents of history, simply a mass to which things happen.

It has been claimed that Scott's films are 'liberal', championing the people over the 'privileged classes' (Schwartz, 2001). It is difficult to see how **Gladiator** really is on the side of masses. It does show certain sections of the ruling elite to be degenerate, but it also suggests that only the upper echelons of society really count. Such a picture is at one with that worldview which sees politics as a clash of a few leading personalities or the economy as the work of a handful of adventurous entrepreneurs, to whom the rest of us owe our living (while they get their much deserved and lavish rewards).

A contrast might be drawn with **Spartacus** whose hero clearly is one of the toiling masses who are championed in the film against their oppressors. Maximus, by contrast, is no 'man of the people'. The images of his farm make clear that he is no peasant toiler but a wealthy landowner, with extensive property and slaves of his own.

The film takes a contradictory stance in another way. In one respect, it endorses a very individualistic worldview. Unlike **Spartacus**, Maximus is on a largely personal mission. His purpose is primarily an individual one, revenge of wrongs against him and his family. At one point he even scrapes off the Roman legion tattoo from his arm with a knife such is his

disillusionment and rejection of his former life. True to the individualistic view of society, it is his personal qualities, his ferocious fighting skills and his dedication to his mission which determine the outcome of the background struggle between senate and Emperor. He is that American ideal: the self-made man (indeed twice over, first leading general, then top gladiator).

At the same time, the film does not ignore the collective. Maximus tells his fellow gladiators that they must stand united or fall. He is shown to honour the memory of his mentor and benefactor Marcus Aurelius and to want a better future for Rome.

Like most historical films, **Gladiator** is quite anachronistic, projecting modern values and concerns back onto the past. It may not be as radical as Stanley Kubrick's **Spartacus** with its overt and very 1960s messages about human dignity and freedom (it was made at the time of the American civil rights movement). None the less, it takes care to present what seems to be a democratic face. Rome's senators, for example, are presented as representatives of the people, worried about the conditions of the poor. Similarly, Maximus and Marcus Aurelius are shown full of angst about that the sacrifices on the battlefield (something for which neither generals nor emperors have been noted in the past).

**Gladiator** does not, however, take the idea of democracy too far. The restored political equilibrium offered at the end of the film is one of power being given back to the senate, i.e. a restoration of rule by and for a very privileged elite. There are few hints of the possibility or desirability of the ordinary people (and certainly not slaves) being enfranchised (unlike **Spartacus**). The dialogue routinely refers to ordinary people as 'the mob' so, clearly, they are not fit to self-rule.

Nor is there any recognition of the long history of class conflict — 'plebs' versus 'patricians' — in ancient Rome. The real Roman world was also deeply divided along the lines of city (Rome)

**NOTES:**

versus countryside, most of whose inhabitants felt that they were being exploited to sustain the bloated metropolis (feelings which, as an alleged farmer, Maximus should have shared).

To be fair, *Gladiator* does not go as far as films like ***Attack of the Clones*** (2002). According to Shone (2004), it endorses the imperial project. By extension, today's 'Pax Americana' is good for the globe just as the empire is shown to be good for the galaxy. Shone, however, may be distorting the narrative of *Gladiator* when he portrays Maximus as simply an ex-insider wanting to be back on the inside. Maximus 'wants out'. He is reminiscent of that American ex-general, President Eisenhower, who duly retired to a farm. Here the film touches upon an image used in many films, the countryside (and small towns) as repositories of peace, simplicity and decency (as opposed to the supposed 'evils' of city life).

Yet Shone's general point stands. Maximus is not shown to have any real critique of Roman imperialism: he just wants to go home. The empire is taken for granted by him and by the film as a whole. At various points, the iconography of *Gladiator* has the look of unchallengeable and unquestionable power (views of Rome through the clouds, monumental buildings, processions, Imperial Eagles, long lines of Praetorian Guards, etc).

The back story provided by text at the start of the film also accepts conventional definitions of 'success', i.e. power, size and conquest. What in reality was oppression and exploitation are cloaked in fine-sounding words about peace and civilisation. The rest of the film fails to ask any probing questions about such 'accomplishments'. It uncritically accepts the dominance of Rome.

Perhaps most significantly *Gladiator* endorses what might be called the 'rotten-apple-spoiling-the-barrel' view of society. In other words, social problems are caused by rogue elements in what, otherwise, is basically a

healthy system. Removal of that odd bad egg (Commodus) will put things to right. Ideas that a dreadful political leader or problems like poverty, war and environmental destruction might be inevitable by-products of a particular social system, or that a more radical re-ordering of society is necessary are, then, not ones to be entertained in this worldview.

## Clash of cultures

Of course, the story of *Gladiator* is set in a time when, from a European perspective, there was but one superpower, Rome. The opening of the film in particular suggests that its military might protected civilisation from barbarity. Today, there is also just one superpower, the USA. Supporters of its role in creating a new world order also see it as the protector of civilised values against the forces of darkness (the old 'evil empire' of the Communist bloc in the past, the new threats posed by Islamic fundamentalism and assorted 'rogue states', more recently).

This is not to say that the makers of *Gladiator* were consciously drawing deliberate parallels between then and now. But it would be incredible if they and their audiences were not, to some extent at least, projecting onto the world of Maximus, hopes, fears and concerns of the present political scene. It is quite reasonable to see allegorical elements in the film.

A number of commentators today have compared the current world order to an 'empire', including Arundhati Roy, Gore Vidal, Michael Hardt and Antonio Negri. At times, there seem to be striking congruencies between then (or, more precisely the imagined world of Imperial Rome) and now. Before battle commences at the start of the film, the barbarians return the severed head of a Roman envoy. The image is reminiscent of footage of the savage treatment of captive Americans in Iraq, Somalia and elsewhere. In turn, the incident seems to justify the overwhelming firepower brought to bear on the Germanic hordes in retaliation. In the film, this 'sorts out'

the barbarian menace (in reality, their lands were never conquered and the frontier 'problem' persisted until Rome itself fell to the Huns and other tribes).

It might also be noted that, in common with other recent films, the armed forces are depicted in a positive light. One of the most sympathetic characters in ***Independence Day*** was an avuncular general whose only desire was to help his President. Maximus and his army too just want to do their duty. In early versions of the screenplay, the army actually intervened to save Rome from tyranny. All this is in striking contrast to those movies that portrayed military leaders as arrogant blunderers and murderous ones at that (some readers may remember General Melchett in the final *Blackadder* TV series as well as generals in ***Paths of Glory*** (1957)). Perhaps it is no coincidence that Ridley Scott comes from a military family.

It should be noted that the binary oppositions of civilised (Rome) and barbaric (the rest) scarcely do justice to the complexities of the real world. There were viable cultures outside Rome during its history such as Carthage and, later, various Celtic societies. Indeed, many of the undoubted achievements of both Greece and Rome were based on Egyptian civilisation. Furthermore, the subsequent 'Dark Ages' after the fall of Rome were in fact not completely 'dark', with various technical, social and cultural accomplishments of their own, just as there was a very dark side to Rome (of which ecological despoilation was the perhaps the least noted but most serious).

It is surely of note that *Gladiator*'s makers went to considerable lengths to get many details about Rome correct but scarcely seem to have bothered when it came to the sequences set in Africa. The locals are made to look like Arabs who are in turn linked to slave trading. The character Juba is given the name of one people, the Amazigh, but not their appearance (they were much fairer skinned than the black actor who plays the part). Middle Eastern

**NOTES:**

music is used for scenes supposedly set in North Africa (where local people did not wear turbans, unlike Proximo). The region was also much more fertile than the desert wasteland shown in the film.

These are very much 'live' issues. The habit of stereotyping an entire culture as depicted in *Gladiator* is that same mindset which, today, sees all Muslims as heartless terrorists or, at least, as potential ones. It might be argued that the character of Juba contradicts such interpretations. This African is depicted as a thoroughly decent, indeed sunny character. Yet he is treated as almost a child who heads off home, without a care in the world, at the end of the film.

Furthermore, (black) Juba owes his freedom to the (white) Maximus. As Fradley (2004) points out, the latter even usurps Juba's position as a victim by pointing out in the dialogue that he (Maximus) has lost everything, unlike his new friend. On the other hand, it might be assumed that a film that has to appeal to multi-racial audiences cannot deal in straightforwardly racist negative stereotypes. The barbaric hordes are, after all, white.

The film strongly endorses family values. In several conversations, Maximus underlines the importance of home and loved ones to him. Even after the death of his own wife, he does not succumb to the temptations of Lucilla. Nor does he become a 'toy boy' for rich women (what Lucilla calls 'rich matrons') as did successful gladiators in real life. He remains loyal to the memory of his wife and child. Outside 'normal' families, trouble and pain loom large (Commodus, it is made clear, is the product of a highly dysfunctional family), but here too *Gladiator* widens its appeal. Part of its audience no longer lives in the conventional nuclear family. They live in surrogate families of the kind celebrated in Friends. After the loss of his blood family, Maximus too finally finds friends.

In terms of other values and messages,

*Gladiator* might seem comparatively muted. Compared to earlier epics like **Ben-Hur**, *Gladiator* makes only fleeting genuflections towards any kind of formal religiosity (though Maximus uses Christian words such as 'Blessed Father' when praying at a pagan shrine). Yet the film certainly does not reject spiritual values per se. After all, Maximus deeply believes in an afterlife. Strong visual and verbal references are made to Elysium throughout the film. *Gladiator*'s appeal might, then, straddle several forces in the world today, including both born-again Christianity and New Age mysticism.

## To kill...or not to kill

It is possible to see the violence depicted in *Gladiator* in two ways (and violence is the core of the film since there is not a great deal of politics, romance or any other ingredient). The film could be seen as a critique of the violent spectacles that not only entertained Roman crowds in the past but also infuse media, sport and other 'entertainments' in the present. This tendency includes factual media, not least their almost voyeuristic coverage of terrorist outrages and other horrors.

The film could be interpreted as a critique of violence in more straightforward ways. Marcus Aurelius is heard condemning his own record of military aggrandisement. Nor is Maximus a cold-hearted killer. He can empathise with the Germanic horde and, in all his battles, he displays no signs of pleasure in violent acts. His own death brings about a release from a world of pain, marked by a shower of flower petals, usually a symbol of peace.

It might also be noted that Maximus resorts to violence after the opening battle scene for sake of vengeance, in other words for the sake of his dead family. In doing so, he is following in the footsteps of **The Outlaw Josey Wales** (1976, a Western in which the hero's family is butchered at the start of the film). It might even be argued that Maximus has had a taste of his

own medicine since, as a general, he presumably would have destroyed many families while on campaign.

Yet other evidence points to a different interpretation. In **Black Hawk Down**, Ridley Scott demonstrated his willingness to indulge in endless carnage, without the contextualising that might explain the violence depicted. The plot of *Gladiator* provides a pretty thin rationale (good man wronged) for the bone-crunching, body-slashing violence that follows. Chariots spectacularly crash but the fate of those on board is ignored as the film cuts to the next round of entertaining thrills and spills. One might reasonably assume that audiences are meant to be enthralled by it, neither repelled nor encouraged to reflect on modern mores.

In line with a very long list of movies, TV shows and computer games, the film depicts violence as the ultimate solution to any problem. Some readers may remember, for example, the TV series, *Kung-Fu*, in which the hero stoically endured all kinds of torment before, in the final few minutes, giving his tormenters a good beating. Maximus too resists pacifically for a few moments on his first day of training at gladiator school but, very quickly, he is dispensing violent punishment to everyone in his path. Indeed, the story is contrived so that he simply has to do this when the alternative (calling in the army to overthrow Commodus) is thwarted. Thus, Maximus is left to sort things out all by himself, sword in hand, in the arena.

**NOTES:**

# Representations of Reality in *Gladiator*

## The trouble with men

*Fight Club*: asserting masculinity

Most movies contain depictions of gender and sexuality. The men and women might be real people or fictional creations. Either way, the way they look and behave, the manner in which they relate to people of the same or opposite sex, how they talk and what they talk about, the things they do and the roles they are shown performing, all construct powerful messages about what it is to be a man or woman (the same too for heterosexual, homosexual or bisexual identities).

There is a body of thought that locates contemporary films, particularly from the 1980s onwards, as an expression of wider 'crisis of masculinity' in society. Allegedly men have lost their traditional roles as breadwinner and protector. Their identities and self-confidence have been undermined in many ways: the destruction of many traditionally 'male' jobs through 'deindustrialisation', the stultifying effects of 'white collar' work, the general replacement of male brawn by machines, and indeed the ability of women to conceive separately from male partners thanks to new fertility techniques.

At the same time, women have won more rights as well as penetrated once male-only preserves (even the golf club!). Men, it is argued, have become progressively disconnected from those two great social institutions: work and family. The crisis is, then, a twin one: loss of old roles and failure to find (or, perhaps, accept) new ones.

The result is male insecurity, devaluation, self-doubt, bewilderment, paranoia, hysteria and even trauma, or so it is claimed. They are impotent in more ways than one. Fradley (2004) spotlights films as varied as *The Sixth Sense* (1999), *The Fugitive* (1993) and *Ransom* (1996) as expressions of modern-man-in-trouble. Previous male characters were often in peril but usually they knew what to do… and confidently did it.

The crisis of masculinity thesis argues, then, that men have been emasculated in real life and that the cinema screen is addressing such changes in society. In some cases, salvation only comes about when men rediscover their manliness in the manner of Brad Pitt in *Fight Club* or Tom Hanks in *Cast Away* (2000). This general phenomenon is also to be found reflected in films that look back on the days when a generation of men really did behave like real men (Fradley cites *Saving Private Ryan* and *Pearl Harbor*).

## Male make-over?

Of course, it is possible to pick holes in such arguments. For a start, in many areas of real life, men still confidently hold sway. Thus, ideas of an all-pervading crisis of masculinity must be questioned. Furthermore, often both men and women (or least those in the ordinary ranks of society) are jointly suffering problems, the causes of which are quite unrelated to gender relationships.

It is not clear, in any case, that significant changes have actually happened in cinematic representations of men and women. In many old films, men were portrayed as anxious, incompetent and/or paranoid (look at the travails of Cary Grant in *Bringing Up Baby* (1938)). Film noir movies often featured weak men suffering at the hands of femme fatales (*Double Indemnity* (1944), etc.). Men in 1950s Westerns often suffered from identity crises and self-doubt (especially in Anthony Mann's films).

The need for a 'remasculinisation' may be suggested in *Fight Club* but not in most movies. Indeed many films question male machismo. In the black comedy *Grosse Pointe Blank* (1997), John Cusack wants to give up the macho violence, while *The Thin Red Line* (1998) and *Three Kings* (1999) continue the tradition of anti-war films.

Yet, there is a substantial body of movies that do fit the 'male crisis' thesis. It is not just refracted through action films. The actor John Cusack has just been mentioned. He spends most of *High Fidelity* (2000) moping around, wondering what he wants in life and fretting over failed relationships. In *Independence Day*, the President (Bill Pullman) is initially shown as in trouble. Indeed his (female) aide pointedly comments on his almost feminine weakness early in the film. He is also shown looking after his daughter, while his wife is out there doing the politics. He only recovers his status and becomes a 'man' again once he turns into a warrior (and indeed a fighter plane 'jock').

## Gladiator and its men

The question is then begged whether Maximus and *Gladiator* deal in the currency of 'tough guise' and other manifestations of the 'crisis in masculinity'. Certainly Maximus possesses all the brooding toughness and rugged individualism of the re-born 'real man'. Like some of the 'redeemed' men note above, he loses his role (general/father) but finds a new one as a veritable *Fight Club* combatant.

Like a true superhero, Maximus is depicted as the object of admiring watchers. He is deferentially watched by his troops at the start of the film. His servant loyally follows him throughout the film (he might have reasonably decided to desert to Quintus). Young Lucius gives the new gladiatorial hero adoring looks while the boy's mother, Lucilla is clearly still smitten by Maximus. Gracchus and his fellow senators give him flattering looks. He is the object of the crowds' cheers. But like some

**NOTES:**

rock-god, he treats his new army of fans at the Colosseum with due disdain. He is Leader of the Pack again and knows it.

Real-life leaders today are usually less disdainful of the masses. They are often seen pointing to people in their audiences. Yet they too want to be shown strutting their stuff across political platforms, conference arenas and military bases. None the less, *Gladiator* would seem to endorse the need for tough, decisive guys at the helm (ones who won't be weak on homeland security and the like).

As noted elsewhere, the audience of the film was fairly evenly split between men and women. It would be reasonable to assume that some women enjoyed looking at Russell Crowe and that he is often positioned to maximum sexual effect (in other words, the 'female gaze' rather than what film theorist Laura Mulvey christened the 'male gaze').

Yet, it would be stretching the argument too far if *Gladiator* were to be primarily characterised as a reflection of an alleged male crisis. Maximus is certainly a very angry, white man (the crisis of masculinity thesis particularly spotlights movies like *Falling Down* (1993) in which men have lost their way in life and are rather cross about it). Yet the revenge narrative owes much to old westerns in which white men like James Stewart and Clint Eastwood lost what was theirs and set out to get those who took it from them.

There is one last theme of male representation in the film: destiny-as-final death. This theme occurs in many genres. Many a Western hero has known that the final outcome could only be death, 'dying with their boots on'. Sometimes they go down fighting like Colonel Custer; at other times, they ride away wounded like Shane. Most of *The Magnificent Seven* (1960) know they are dancing with death.

Redemption does not, of course, always come

from death. But it often involves sacrifice. This might be a matter of ego: surrendering individuality and bonding with other males as in *The Shawshank Redemption* (1994) or many a Howard Hawk's movie (as happens with Proximo's gladiators). Alternatively it could be actual physical suffering as in *Fight Club*. Maximus certainly suffers en route to the final confrontation.

This theme, especially its more lethal variant, is perhaps most developed in the movies of Sam Peckinpah. Terence Butler's study of the director (1979) appropriately uses the title of 'Crucified Heroes'. Peckinpah's men, be they a platoon on the Russian front in World War II or a cowboy gang in *The Wild Bunch* (1969), gladly and indeed almost erotically go to meet the hail of bullets awaiting them.

The hero, Maximus, may not be actually crucified but he is a dead man on leave, as *Gladiator*'s prologue hints. He could have taken the soft option and made his peace with Commodus. Instead, he is burdened by duty and destiny for which he duly suffers. He certainly achieves his goal but the fruits of victory are only tasted in death. Of course, his death may be just a crude appeal to audience sentiment. But perhaps there really are 'no more heroes anymore' or, more precisely, ones who can be allowed to live to a ripe old age. The crisis of the modern male hero is that he is a tortured soul. Maximus has been effectively emasculated by Commodus before his last battle so, possibly, only death will become him.

## Gladiator and its women

Representation of women in the movie is more a matter of omission. Female characters are conspicuous by their comparative absence, with the obvious exception of Lucilla. Her main function of the film is to provide a 'love interest' as well as underline the beastliness of Commodus who is shown to have unwholesome desires for her (and possibly her son too).

Early in the film, her father is heard wishing

that she were a man. Such scripting could be taken different ways. It might be read as a tribute to Lucilla's strength of character, a recognition of the rules of male primogeniture or as another reassertion of masculinity by the film. It might be noted that the script has a worthy literary pedigree at this point since thoughts similar to those of Marcus Aurelius are in texts as diverse as *King Lear*, *Ivanhoe* and *Lord of the Rings*. Perhaps the real Henry VIII might have muttered such words about his daughter Elizabeth (who, apparently, wished she had the body of a man).

Such representation would seem quite stereotypical. Lucilla suffers a conventional crisis of women in films: a conflict in which she is forced to choose either Maximus and support the conspiracy against Commodus or do her motherly duty and protect her son. In fact, *Gladiator* drastically bends the historical stick in this direction since the real Lucilla was quite a feisty character. She actively plotted against Commodus and paid with her life. In the film, Lucilla lives on. Perhaps, as a woman, she thus symbolises some kind of continuity, linking the generations and almost guaranteeing a legitimate succession.

The only other woman of any significance is the virtually unseen wife of Maximus. The fact that she is raped, not just killed (a point that Commodus verbally drives home) is the kind of motivating device that makes a virile hero like Maximus even more desirous of vengeance.

In passing it might be noted that *Gladiator* omits another group of women: female gladiators. The existence of several decrees banning such fighters suggests that there were such combatants as does somewhat more tentative archaeological evidence. But in the male world of *Gladiator* they clearly had no place. There is actually one female charioteer (in the Tunic Wars re-enactment), but she gets cut in half.

## Sexual nature

*Gladiator* not only addresses gender

**NOTES:**

relationships. It also dips its sandals into the waters of sexual orientation. Indeed virtually the only joke in the film is Proximo's complaint about having being sold 'queer giraffes'. It is suggested that Senator Gracchus has a young man as a partner but, otherwise, the film would appear resolutely heterosexual.

Yet the film does put strong emphasis on male bonding. Furthermore, it seems reasonable to point to a certain homoerotic element in the sight of so much bare male flesh on display and of (good looking) men bashing each other. Compared to, say, **Braveheart**, heterosexual love and romance are very low key. William Wallace has not just one but two great loves in his film life but Maximus remains strictly celibate.

There is nothing new in such representations. Back in 1938, Errol Flynn's **Robin Hood and his Merry Men** were happily having adventures in Sherwood Forest unencumbered by women. In the 1962 **Lawrence of Arabia** the eponymous hero similarly roamed the Arabian desert in the company of men. Audiences have seen men bonding in mental health wards (**One Flew Over the Cuckoo's Nest**, 1975) and out in the backwoods (**Deliverance**, 1972, which featured a homosexual rape which instantly triggers the film's most violent reaction).

Not surprisingly it happens most often on the battlefield. Young men coming of age need to bond too (e.g. **Stand By Me**, 1986). In **Jaws**, it seems as if the three male characters cannot wait to dump domestic responsibilities and set sail together (some male sparring included). Buddy movies also feature buddies who are usually men (though usually in chalk-and-cheese varieties just as in TV's *Starsky and Hutch*).

So sights like Maximus and his band of brothers are not unusual at the cinema. Whether there is some gay sub-text remains a matter of speculation. But it is fair to wonder whether the repeated assertion of a tough masculinity could be said to conceal some deeper insecurities and uncertainties about

identity and values, both within the text itself and its viewers.

---

**NOTES:**

**'The range is good'** (Maximus in *Gladiator*)

**Most movies have a number of discrete audiences. Commercially, the most important is obviously the film-watching public, be it in the cinema or at home, viewing movies on TV channels, video and DVD. Film audiences might be further sub-divided into the more casual viewer and the hard-core fan.**

Another audience is composed of professional film critics. Some will influence, in turn, that first audience, especially those debating whether it is really worth going to see a particular film. Such criticism varies wildly, from shallow hype to in-depth analysis, usually reflecting the readership or viewer.

Another audience is composed of judges at the various film festivals and competitions. *Gladiator* did well here, garnering five Oscars at the seventy-third Academy Awards in 2001 — Best Picture, Actor in a leading role (Russell Crowe), Costume Design, Sound and Visual Effects. Beforehand, in Britain, it won five BAFTAs, including Best Film. Russell Crowe also picked up the Best Actor Award from the American Broadcast Film Critics Association which also chose Joaquin Phoenix as Best Supporting Actor while John Mathieson won the Best Cinematography award.

Such acclaim clearly will not harm box office prospects. Indeed, it might partly explain why *Gladiator* enjoyed extra 'shelf life' in the cinemas compared to its main rivals. That said, the 'Oscar effect' usually has more impact on the prospects of small-budget movies which, otherwise, might quickly disappear from view.

## High-brow, low-brow, no-brow?

Though individual critics may influence certain groups among cinema-goers, there is something of a chasm between what critics as a whole rate and what appeals to the general public. *Gladiator* illustrates this gap. It was one of the top ten highest grossing movies of

2000 in the USA (the others were *How the Grinch Stole Christmas*, *Mission: Impossible II*, *The Perfect Storm*, *Meet the Parents*, *X-Men*, *Scary Movie*, *What Lies Beneath*, *Dinosaur* and *Erin Brockovich*).

Perusal of serious film journals and other sources of 'cinéaste' opinion might find some positive noises about the last film in that list. *Gladiator* too was received quite respectfully. The other eight were largely ignored in favour of a mix of small 'indie' and foreign language films. Indeed, one might distinguish 'films' (what critics highly rate) from 'movies' (what goes down well with the public).

This gulf might be explained in different ways. It could be argued that some films need to be 'worked at', thus not appealing to people looking for easy-on-the-brain entertainment. However, the most obvious explanation is the sheer power of marketing among the general population. It is a force that should not be exaggerated since some heavily marketed movies do not succeed at the box office. But it would be equally foolish to downplay its impact.

## Critical opinion

It is not hard to imagine how *Gladiator* might have been torn to shreds by professional critics. After all, the film is far from rich in either plot or characters. Visually it is certainly slick but takes no risks in either camerawork or editing. Yet, the film received generally positive responses in serious 'broadsheets' like *The Guardian* and journals such as *Sight and Sound*. Perhaps there is strong awareness of film history and genre conventions among such reviewers. Scott's achievement in reviving a rather moribund genre would therefore be likely to attract praise. Similarly, his ability to create a convincing world on screen might also be relished by those who spend much of their time having to watch unpersuasive dross.

Alongside traditional print-based reviewing, there is now the thriving virtual community of

web reviewers. *Filmink*, for example, declared that Crowe 'manages to upstage an awesome cast in an awesome movie with an awesome budget'. Another site, *STST* praised the 'fire, brimstone and fury' of Scott's action scenes, adding that Crowe's presence transformed 'what could have been just a gormless action movie with a big budget … into an amazing epic'.

Box office takings are the most obvious guide to the public's opinions about a film, although, of course, there will be many more people who saw *Gladiator* on video, DVD and TV screenings. It dominated cinema screens in America at its opening weekend, selling more tickets than the next seven films combined and earning $34.8 million. Those figures perhaps do not fully illuminate the appeal of the film.

For a start, there were major basketball games on television at the same time. It was rated 'R' in America (equivalent to '15' in the UK), thus excluding some potential viewers from its audience. It was also quite a long film, running for more than two and half hours, something else that could have discouraged some cinema-goers. Yet *Gladiator*'s appeal was such that these factors did not harm total attendance figures.

Most significantly, the film had 'legs', demonstrating strong staying power at the cinema. This can be seen by comparing its first weekend takings with its overall gross (the former was 18.5% of the final takings). It is also evident when that first weekend is compared with the second. In this case, takings did fall as might be expected but only by −29%. This might seem a high figure but it was much less than that for, say, *The Mummy* which fell by − 43% (often called the 'burn-out' factor).

Audiences responded strongly outside the USA. Its overseas box office earnings were much higher at $266,694,000 than the American total of $187,670,866. Globally it

**NOTES:**

came second only to ***Mission Impossible II***. According to figures from the Lumière database, some 29,748,471 people across Europe saw the film. It was most popular in the UK, followed by Spain, France and Germany. Clearly the strategy discussed above under 'Building an Audience' reaped dividends.

## Assessing the response

It is difficult, however, to interpret public responses beyond simple totals. One might suspect that ***Gladiator*** was a 'man's movie'. Figures from CAVIAR Ireland cite male/female audiences as respectively 58%/42%. The opening weekend audiences in the USA also had a male bias. Yet, according to one of the people involved in ***Gladiator***'s distribution interviewed by King (2002), the balance became 50/50 as weeks went by.

According to the Irish data, ***Gladiator*** appealed more to people in social categories C2DE (54% of overall audience), whereas films generally have a slightly higher appeal in the ABC1 groups compared to the general population. Of the Irish audience, 52% were aged 15–24 and only 18% over 34. This last figure is slightly surprising since 37% of the Irish audience for ***The Patriot*** was over 34. Less surprisingly, a more 'intellectual' film like ***American Beauty*** enjoyed stronger support from people over 25 than did ***Gladiator***.

It is even harder to explain why all these people went to see ***Gladiator***. There are a myriad of websites where fans record their verdicts but it is impossible to assess just how representative such opinions are. A number of points suggest themselves: some are fairly self-evident, while others are more speculative. It would be rather surprising if people said that they enjoyed ***Gladiator*** for its labyrinthine plot or its deep meditations on the human condition.

## The wow factor

Probably the greatest pleasure for most viewers in ***Gladiator*** is sheer spectacle. Audiences can immerse themselves in over two hours' worth

of visual delights. They include the adrenalin rush of the opening battle, the exotic world of an Arab slave camp and the stunning recreation of the city of Rome. The sight of the (reconstructed) Colosseum in all its gigantic majesty is central to such visual pleasures.

Much of the spectacle is of course death and destruction which audiences can vicariously enjoy from the safety of their cinema seats. For the most part, it is anonymous barbarians and faceless gladiators who are being smitten. Otherwise, it is someone getting his just desserts. At the movie's climax, our hero emerges from the 'valley of darkness' beneath the Colosseum to strike down the tyrant Commodus.

It might be asked whether these pleasures might have been so enjoyable if it had been Commodus committing all the slaughter. As it is, audiences can easily savour a guiltless frisson as Maximus slays one opponent after another with great vengeance and furious anger as they cross his righteous path. The good feelings engendered by moral justice being seen to be done and purely visceral pleasures thus go hand in hand.

## Character appeal

Much of the appeal of a movie will also come from the characters who parade through its story as well as the stars who play them. First and foremost, there is Maximus. The character certainly has many of the qualities of a popular hero — tough, authoritative but still decent, loyal, tenacious, supremely capable yet modest, blessed with good looks, sharp mind and strong muscle, formidable fighter but also loving father and husband. Both as general and gladiator, our hero remains true to himself.

The script emphasises that all he wants to do is quit fighting and return home. There is added poignancy that he is robbed of that dream. His misfortune is truly undeserved which is another reason why many viewers will identify strongly with him and enjoy the film all the

more. At the same time, the audience is continually reminded of his heroism. Though his progress might at times seem implausible, it is still believable in terms of the overall narrative of ***Gladiator***. There are not too many coincidences and plot contrivances to insult the audience's intelligence.

The Maximus character may appeal to audiences in other ways. There is a strong streak of individualism, even a certain solitude. He keeps his distance from his fellow gladiators and his former lover, Lucilla. At times he even despairs. Possibly this may reinforce his appeal to modern audiences, among whom collective values have, to some extent, been supplanted by much more individualistic ones.

The character of Commodus also has a multi-layered appeal. Most obvious is his role as traditional 'bad guy'. His wickedness progressively worsens over the course of the film. Both his machinations and eventual comeuppance can by enjoyed by audiences. Yet, he might also have a more modern appeal. The image of a power-crazed dictator cynically manipulating the masses is one which will resonate with many sections of the audience. Better still, unlike Stalin, Hitler and Mao, he is prepared to do his own dirty work. He is no cowardly villain lurking in the shadows. This Emperor can fight like a gladiator (as Commodus did in real life).

An additional point of appeal might be feelings of empathy evoked by the dilemma faced by Lucilla (how to protect her son). That she stands by Maximus may also boost the film's romantic appeal for some viewers, if not others (who might find this part of the story rather corny). That said, ***Gladiator*** is very much a male-dominated film. There are no tough cases like Ripley in ***Alien*** or Sarah Connor in the ***Terminator*** films.

The gladiatorial entrepreneur Promixo is a familiar character. He is certainly a rogue and yet, deep down, he can be both loyal and kind-

**NOTES:**

hearted. His better qualities emerge later in the film, offering the familiar consolation of a character redeeming himself. Even the treacherous Quintus who initially betrays Maximus manages to redeem himself too, another heart-warming sight.

## Star power

A star for today: tough yet vulnerable

Russell Crowe probably brought with him many fans, whose ranks were further swelled by his performance. 'Fandom' is an elusive entity. Its members are certainly enthusiastic, if not obsessive, in their allegiances. An article in *The Charlotte Observer* (1 October 2000) quotes a 40-year-old woman, a public relations executive, who has seen *Gladiator* ten times. *Montreal Gazette* writer Lisa Fitterman claims that women do not want Sensitive New Age Guys (SNAGs). 'I am beyond hot. I want heat. I want Russell Crowe,' she says. Believers in gender equality might feel uncomfortable with women who say they want 'take-charge heroes who can take care of us', in the words of another Crowe fan.

To the traditional virtues of a male hero, Crowe manages to add a gentler, more 'feminine' side. It is in marked contrast to the older tradition of male action film stars like John Wayne and Kirk Douglas. Machismo is still alive and kicking in modern society but, alongside it, have emerged other values and lifestyles, emphasising co-operation, tolerance and empathy.

Crowe also enjoys a certain youthfulness which other action stars like Mel Gibson and Bruce Willis no longer possess. He exhibits both an air of intelligence and physical strength (unlike, say, Sly Stallone). Perhaps many men and women share a need to believe in a man who is good-hearted but can also 'handle' himself. Add a 'colourful' private life (drunken brawls, etc.) and the contribution from Crowe to the film's appeal becomes stronger still.

The presence of Danish actress Connie Nielsen as Lucilla also strikes a certain balance in terms of audience appeal. She has the traditional blonde good looks yet possesses strength also. The film's appeal to older sections of the audience was heightened by the presence of a slate of veteran actors — Oliver Reed, Richard Harris, Derek Jacobi and David Hemmings. There is always a certain enjoyment in seeing such people again and usually they can be relied upon to deliver solid performances. There is the additional curiosity value of a film in which one of the main actors died in the filming. Much of *Gladiator*'s publicity focused on how modern technology allowed the dead Oliver Reed to 'live on' during the film's making.

A number of fan sites also responded to the director, not just the stars. One, *Ain't It Cool*, responded thus: 'This is the Ridley Scott that we fanboys and girls drool over…*Gladiator* is a great cool film.' It is Scott's reputation for style, detail and pace that seems to be what is admired.

## Subject matter

Some subjects seem to have enduring appeal for film audiences — dinosaurs, vampires, psychopaths, hard-boiled detectives and, if we take the total number of films ever made, the Wild West. The Roman empire too would appear to possess considerable stating power in terms of its appeal. As historian Tristram Hunt has noted (*Observer*, 1 August 2004), 'the immorality, corruption and vanity of Rome proved a beguiling cultural spectacle. Today, we continue to be entranced by the fatal romance of Rome's collapse.'

It is not just the larger-than-life quality of Julius Caesar, Caligula and Spartacus or the drama of chariot races and crucifixions. There is something about Rome itself that speaks to us today. We live in troubled times, not unlike those depicted in *Gladiator*. One 'empire' rules the world: the USA. But it is challenged on many sides, not least by the 'barbarian' forces of terrorism. Not long ago, another seemingly invincible empire, the Soviet bloc, dramatically collapsed. The rise and fall of empires is, then, a theme of great contemporary relevance. This is not to be say that *Gladiator* is some sophisticated political treatise. Rather, it offers the thrills and spills of an action blockbuster plus a storyline that resonates with contemporary concerns.

Further, within many ruling elites, not least those in the USA, all kinds of machinations seem to be afoot, just as in the Rome of Marcus Aurelius and Commodus. The success of Michael Moore's *Fahrenheit 9/11* (2004) suggests that many members of the public are interested in the political skulduggery of those in charge of society. The idea of intervention by the military to 'sort things out' (as considered by Maximus in *Gladiator*) is also a live one.

At the same time, many people still seem to retain faith in untainted heroes, as demonstrated by the success of maverick political candidates like Arnold

**NOTES:**

# Responses to *Gladiator*

Schwarzenegger, who came riding to the rescue of the state of California. Incorruptible Maximus stands in marked contrast to not only the degenerate Commodus but also the schemers of Rome's senate.

The last point should not be taken too far, however. Certainly individual senators are shown to be wheelers and dealers. But the institution of the senate itself is essentially depicted in a good light. The soon-to-die Marcus Aurelius speaks of it with respect. Senator Gracchus becomes a more attractive figure as the film progresses. The reason may be that the idea of a Republic is still a positive one in many countries and none more than the USA (where much state architecture is based on Rome). At an allegorical level, *Gladiator* endorses the ideal of the Republic.

*Gladiator* could also be enjoyed as a critique of celebrity culture and show business, past and present. The Colosseum scenes look like a modern sports event and are filmed as if being broadcast on TV (Cyrino, 2004). As if in acknowledgement, *Gladiator*'s music was used to score the broadcasts of the 2002 National Football League season in the USA.

Maximus becomes a star but his fame rests on crowd-pleasing entertainment soaked in blood and gore. He himself is shown to be scornful of his fans, even throwing a sword at the Colosseum's equivalent of the VIP boxes that now adorn many modern stadia. Today's public itself seems uneasy about stardom. It buys celebrity gossip publications, watches talk shows and turns out in big numbers at gala premieres. Celebrity endorsements now sell all kinds of products from crisps to trainers. Stars even command attention when they deign to pronounce on political matters. Yet, there is also resentment, something reflected in the widespread pleasure taken when a celebrity falls from grace. Stardom is, then, a fickle thing. As an allegory, *Gladiator* manages to touch on many aspects of this strange phenomenon.

## Comfort appeal

The story itself offers a very reassuring message, one of added appeal in today's complex and troubled times. The hero gets his revenge in the end, the 'bad guy' gets his just desserts, democracy (of a very limited sort) triumphs over dictatorship. It resonates with one of the most powerful of modern belief systems, namely that people make their own luck and that individuals can make a difference.

When the going gets tough, tough Maximus certainly gets going! Generations of movies, especially Westerns, have schooled audiences into understanding, expecting and, indeed, appreciating such heroics. Transformed into an underdog, always a favourite character, not just in film but also in sport and elsewhere, Maximus overcomes one setback after another until he obtains his chance for revenge.

Of course, in *Gladiator*, the hero dies at the end of the movie. Yet a feel-good ending is still contrived. The script makes clear that Maximus longs to be with his family, in Heaven if not down on Earth, while, in a coda at the film's close, the African gladiator Juba is shown happily heading home.

There will be viewers who found all this rather corny. Yet, an alternative storyline (e.g. Maximus surviving and becoming emperor, marrying Lucilla and becoming stepfather to her son Lucius, elements of which were indeed present in the first screenplay) might have turned acceptable corn into unpleasant syrup. In any case, it cannot be stressed too strongly that what might be cliché-ridden to some may be accessible and pleasingly familiar entertainment to others.

Generally, the film had strong consonant values: it fitted well with the deep beliefs and specific opinions of large sections of its audience. It is not just that it had a hero who could overcome all adversity or a villain who got what he deserved. It suggested that,

through the reunion of Maximus with his family in an afterlife, life can even overcome death.

## Other points of appeal

To underline the main point being made here, a successful film will have many ways of appealing to different audiences. *Gladiator* cannot rival the somewhat blatant attempts of a film like **Independence Day** to be inclusive of just about every ethnic and other minority group. Yet, it does include an attractive and strong non-white character in the person of Juba (Djimon Hounsou). In the form of bright-eyed Lucius there is also a character with whom youthful sections of the audience might identify (apart from hero Russell Crowe).

The locations too are suitably varied from dark forests to shimmering deserts, adding interest value. Much of the imagery of *Gladiator* has special appeal. The remains of the Roman empire dot many landscapes across Europe, from Hadrian's Wall in England to surviving arenas in many towns in southern Europe. Such sites attract millions of visitors, testifying to the popularity of the Roman past.

Gladiatorial combat itself seems to exercise a hold on popular imagination. The UK History Channel routinely refers to fighter pilots of the two World Wars as 'gladiators'. It is even reflected in the pastiche in the popular TV series *American Gladiators*. The battle scene at the start of *Gladiator* also connects to mass culture. Many viewers will have been to re-enactments of old battles and will relish the sight of such combat being staged on what seems to be a much more realistic and grander scale. The sight of fire drenching the trees where the barbarian forces have grouped (another historical inaccuracy) might also connect to actuality footage of napalm igniting whole forests in Vietnam.

Other elements of the iconography of *Gladiator* also have their own resonance. The image of a hero proudly standing alone is one

**NOTES:**

which has been used many times in paintings, photographs, comics, films and television. Indeed Maximus, positioned with the Colosseum in the background, in turn became an iconic image, being recycled, for example, by Fray Bentos, the makers of canned meat, with a somewhat portly gentleman taking the place of Russell Crowe. It was echoed to some extent on the BBC's advertising for its coverage of the 2004 Olympics with the sportsman hero defying malevolent gods to reach an adoring audience in a Colosseum-like arena.

## Men bonding

Some areas of possible appeal can only be speculative. Like many action films, *Gladiator* contains a strong element of male bonding. Somewhat implausibly, Maximus manages to forge a team out of disparate characters with whom he finds himself in the arena. Thereafter, they remain loyal to each other, even sacrificing themselves so that Maximus can (unsuccessfully) attempt an escape later in the film.

The film does not go as far as *Jaws* whose second half becomes a tale of three-men-in-a-boat, free from the encumbrance of women. Nor is there the same homoerotic undertow of *Spartacus* (especially evident in the restored version of Kubrick's masterpiece). Indeed, none of Scott's films match Sam Peckinpah's repeated explorations of men-in-danger. Yet, it remains a definite feature of *Gladiator*.

The homoerotic appeal of Italian 'beefcake' movies in the 1960s has been noted above. It is difficult to evaluate *Gladiator* in these terms. One website, www.aboutgaymovies.com, makes no mention of the film. However, *PlanetOut* enthuses about 'half-naked brawny men on display' in the movie ('Homo Maximus'). Perhaps beauty is indeed in the eye of the beholder.

Whether its appeal has increased in a society where, according to some, there is a 'crisis in masculinity' (loss of traditional male roles combined with increased female assertiveness) must remain an open question. The popularity of films like *Fight Club* among young men might suggest that the answer will, to some extent, be a positive one

This is not to say that *Gladiator*'s appeal in these respects is confined to one gender. Intense personal relationships are deeply powerful elements in mass culture, both male and female. Though there is no conventional love story in the film compared to, say, *Titanic*, there are various kinds of affection on display. There is the father-son relationship of Maximum and Marcus Aurelius, the love of Maximus for his wife and daughter, the revived feelings for him on the part of Lucilla, and, as discussed above, there is the bond of friendship formed among the gladiators. There is certainly much action but the film-makers have been sufficiently sensitive to other parts of mass culture not to leave out the heart strings.

It would be one-sided to discuss only positive responses. Most negative reaction conceded that the film is impressive as a sensory experience (even worthy of purely technical appreciation), but remains a meal devoid of real nourishment: much style but little substance. 'Eye candy' is a typical comment. Such opinions pop up in several contributions to websites set up by film fans. It must be noted as well that many, many more millions of people remain utterly indifferent either way, never bothering to watch the film either at the cinema or on TV.

But whether it is judged in box office takings or in the competition to screen it on TV, *Gladiator* remains an undeniably popular film. Perhaps the secret of its success with different people is that it has something for, if not everyone, certainly many types of audience. One can focus on different elements with repeat viewings. Such qualities probably will give *Gladiator* a longer 'shelf life' than many of its contemporaries.

**NOTES:**

# Classroom Worksheets

The following study questions sometimes ask you to think about films other than Gladiator. If you haven't seen them, you can probably find plenty of details, including, in some cases, screen stills, in the books listed in the bibliography. There are many useful websites. For general details of a film, try the Internet Movie Database (www.imdb.com/). In many cases, it will be worth looking at www.filmsite.org/ which also has a guide to film genres and lists of genre movies. The 'Greatest Films' website (www.the-numbers.com/charts/today.html) is good for box office information. To see what critics said about a film, follow the links at www.rottentomatoes.com/. The reviews not only give you an insight into critical opinion but usually contain valuable information about production, film style and so forth. The on-line encyclopaedia (http://en.wikipedia.org/wiki/Main_Page) has many entries about film genres, national cinema, studios, directors, actors and individual films. If you want to search for magazine and newspaper articles, try the following two sites: www.questia.com/Index.jsp and www.findarticles.com/.

# Genre

1. If potential audiences for *Gladiator* heard that it was an 'epic', what expectations would that term be likely to trigger in their minds? To what extent does *Gladiator* confirm those thoughts and to what extent does it contain surprises?

2. What conventions does *Gladiator* share with films like *Troy* (2004), *Alexander* (2004), *King Arthur* (2004)? In what ways is it different?

3. Many Roman epics were made before *Gladiator*. How and why had the conventions of the genre changed since the last wave of epics in the 1950s and 1960s (*El Cid, Ben-Hur* and *Cleopatra*).

4. The most direct forerunner of *Gladiator* was *The Fall of the Roman Empire* (1964) which was based on the same real historical events and characters. In what ways and why were the two films quire different in form and style?

5. In traditional Hollywood crime thrillers like *The Public Enemy* (1931) and *White Heat* (1949), the narrative is often structured around the rise and fall of a gangster. How do epics like *Gladiator* differ?

6. Are there typical ingredients of an epic beyond just large-scale spectacle?

# Classroom Worksheets

## Narrative

1. Film stories are usually based on particular characters and the changes in their attitudes, behaviour and relationships to other characters over the course of the movie. How do Maximus, Quintus and Proximus change during the story of *Gladiator*?

2. Try to develop a different narrative for *Gladiator*, preserving the core story intact. You might consider telling the story from the point of view of a particular character or altering the sequence of time through devices such as flashbacks.

3. In what is sometimes called the Classical Hollywood tradition, events in stories have clear causes and equally clear consequences while the characters are usually driven by understandable and obvious motives. How true to these conventions is the narrative of *Gladiator*?

4. What are the major decisive turning points in the plot of *Gladiator*?

5. In what ways is the ending of *Gladiator* anticipated in the prologue and opening battlefield scene?

6. To what extent, does the structure of 'equilibrium-disruption-restoration of equilibrium' apply to the narrative of *Gladiator*? You might also try to imagine some alternative endings that nonetheless bring closure to the story.

## Representation

1. Older generations of historians sometimes wrote about 'the glory that was Rome'. What picture of Roman civilisation is painted by *Gladiator*?

2. Ridley Scott's film *Black Hawk Down* (2002) was criticised for depicting non-white peoples as faceless and worthless cannon fodder, just there in the film to be spectacularly blown away in a hail of American bullets and bombs. How does *Gladiator* depict non-Roman peoples?

3. Many critics noted that films like *Alien* (1979) and *The Terminator* (1984) gave female characters much more positive and dynamic roles. Does *Gladiator* break free from or conform to conventional stereotypes of male and female roles?

4. *Lord of the Rings* (2001-03) was significantly restructured to build up the female parts. Try to map out how *Gladiator* might be similarly altered if it were to be re-made.

5. How far can *Gladiator* be said to be about contemporary global politics, with the story of ancient Rome being used as a metaphor for current issues, especially so-called 'Pax Americana' (i.e. the dominant role played by the USA today)?

6. To what extent does *Gladiator* legitimise or condemn the use of violence?

# Classroom Worksheets

## Authorship

1. What has *Gladiator* got in common with other films directed by Ridley Scott?

2. To what extent was *Gladiator* a departure for Ridley Scott when compared to his previous films?

3. Should Ridley Scott be seen as a really skilled technician or as a true film 'auteur'?

4. What other individuals and groups could be said to have contributed significantly to giving *Gladiator* its style and content? The film's credits may suggest some other 'authors' of the movie.

5. Is there such a thing as 'a DreamWorks film', i.e. one that bears the distinctive stamp of that studio?

6. Is there any way it could be argued that Russell Crowe puts a personal stamp on films in which he stars?

## Institutions — the Film Industry and Its Audiences

1. What factors might have persuaded decision-makers in the film industry that there would be a market for a film like *Gladiator*?

2. To what extent is *Gladiator* a product of the modern movie business in terms of its genesis, funding, production, distribution and exhibition compared to films made in the so-called Golden Age of Hollywood (e.g. movies like the 1925 *Ben-Hur* or the 1938 *Adventures of Robin Hood*)?

3. What might explain the box office success of *Gladiator*? You will have to bear in mind what other films were in circulation or about to be released when the film was being screened. Has it got any 'unique selling points' or at least some very distinctive points of appeal?

4. Many kinds of people watch movies. How was *Gladiator* constructed and marketed to appeal across different audience segments?

5. Film 'franchises' like *Star Wars* (1977–83; 1999–2005) build upon prequels and sequels. Try to think of ways in which the movie business could squeeze new films out of *Gladiator*.

6. It is quite common for films to be sold again to audiences under the marketing tool of the 'Director's Cut' and other such labels. What would you add or delete if you were to make changes to *Gladiator* to increase its appeal?

7. What do you consider to have been the most significant choices made during the pre-production, production, post-production and distribution stages of *Gladiator*'s 'life'?

8. Imagine you are discussing with a friend who has not seen *Gladiator* whether s/he should make sure to see it. List both positive and negative points you would make.

9. *Gladiator* appears on a number of fan-created websites. What kind of things appeal to such enthusiasts about the film?

10. Ridley Scott's *Blade Runner* (1982) has become something of a 'cult classic'. Does *Gladiator* have any qualities that might earn such a status? If so, why? If not, why not?

# Appendix: Roman History and *Gladiator*

There were various battles between Roman armies and the Germanic tribes on the empire's frontiers. The notion of a last, great battle is, however, a conceit, merely serving the narrative's need to switch attention from the military to the political. Emperor Marcus Aurelius *did* die on that frontier near the Danube, probably from the diseases that plagued armies of the time. It might be noted that he savagely persecuted Christians, something at variance with the gentle sage depicted in *Gladiator*. This change conveniently created a wise father figure for Maximus.

Marcus Aurelius was succeeded by his son Commodus as planned by his father (contrary to the film). Commodus simply had no reason to murder his father. The new Emperor was indeed idle and dissolute, more interested in orgies and violent spectacles in the arena than imperial duties. He was actually married at the time *Gladiator* is set (and had blonde hair). He had plenty of political experience — he wasn't simply the playboy of the film. He was also a skilful fighter in his right as shown in the film, regularly appearing as a gladiator himself (though one wonders whether his opponents may have been told to concede victory since he was Emperor). He became increasingly mentally unbalanced though one doubts whether Commodus ever uttered lines like 'This vexes me. I'm very vexed!' The numerous murders he perpetrated against leading families was to provoke the backlash that in turn killed him. His death was widely celebrated.

Lucilla existed too, 12 years older than Commodus and had been married to her father's co-Emperor Lucius Verus who had also died. She took numerous lovers, contradicting the film's image of a dutiful and somewhat chaste mother. However, she did actively plot against her brother before being banished and then executed.

There was a Gracchus but during the time of the Roman Republic, some 300 years before the movie. He was a representative of the ordinary masses, a Plebian Tribune, and therefore an opponent of the senators, the group to which the film's Gracchus is shown to belong. Roman politics were somewhat more complicated than Hollywood suggests.

Maximus is, of course, a fictional character. However, there was one Emperor, Diocletian, who, like Maximus, came from outside the nobility but won his Emperor's friendship, was made his general and then named his heir, duly becoming Emperor himself. By contrast, the real general of Marcus Aurelius on the German frontier tried to usurp the throne but was killed by his own troops. There was, apparently, a senator called Maximus who was executed by Commodus.

There were also Emperors who came from the Provinces. One from Spain was Hadrian, he of the famous Wall. Indeed, Marcus Aurelius himself, though born in Rome, came from a family of Spanish aristocratic descent. Some critics of *Gladiator* make much of Maximus 'The Spaniard' being an outsider yet the upper classes of the Roman empire, especially around the Mediterranean, were culturally quite Romanised.

In reality, there would have been no need for Proximo to have a training school in Africa. He could have legally operated in Rome or somewhere else on the Italian peninsula. This relocation does serve the narrative in that the journey made by Maximus thereby becomes all the more arduous.

There was, of course, a real Colosseum, though it was not known by that name until the Middle Ages. The largest amphitheatre in the Roman world, it was inaugurated in AD 80. It had four tiers and could seat 60,000 spectators. They came to watch professional gladiators as well as groups sentenced for slaughter such as slaves, criminals and persecuted Christians. All kinds of animals were slaughtered in what amounted to biocide: bears, lions, panthers, elephants, rhinoceroses, giraffes and ostriches all perished, rendering them extinct in certain regions.

There seems to be some conflict in the evidence about death rate in the gladiatorial arena. On the one hand, it is plausibly argued that, like today's sporting heroes, gladiators were very valuable property, too expensive to kill off. Yet it is also recorded that in the first two weeks after the Colosseum's opening, some 2,000 gladiators were killed in it. The games were also used as a means of disposing of unwanted slaves, prisoners of war, religious heretics and criminals. Their death rate would have been very high.

Certainly the top gladiators were stars and rich women would want their 'favours' as *Gladiator* suggests (which explains why some free men signed up to fight). The historical accuracy of the 'thumbs down' sign has been widely questioned (a diagonal gesture is often suggested as more accurate).

The gladiatorial contests depicted in the film ignore the rules that governed armour and weaponry. In particular, for the sake of stressing the obstacles Maximus has to overcome, he is shown in confrontations with opponents against whom he would appear to have no chance. In reality, it was thought better entertainment to stage fair fights, albeit with gladiators armed with different but equally dangerous weapons.

The film also emphasises large-scale re-enactments at the expense of the far more common but less cinematically spectacular one-to-one contests. That said, there were some huge battles staged, including ones set at sea. (Perhaps modern viewers might have suspended their disbelief at that point.)

What is not in doubt is that the Roman masses loved the games just as the film depicts. They did, however, possess some religious symbolism, something that the Romans had

**NOTES:**

inherited from the funeral rites practised by the Etruscans. The ideas of honouring the Gods as well as personal atonement were important ones in the Roman belief system (which would have included chariot races in their honour and the slaughtering of animals). Though it is widely noted that such spectacles were used to placate the masses, the latter might have felt some sense of empowerment. Indeed, emperors competed for the favour of the masses by putting on the 'best' show in town. In the violent world of the time, the games would not have been seen as shocking as they might be to modern eyes.

The battle scene at the start of the film does capture the scale of Roman operations. Correctly, organisation and discipline are shown to be the key to military success. However, the film's need for spectacle led to the employment on the battlefield of huge mechanical weapons like siege catapults that probably would have been too cumbersome to haul through the forests of Germania.

The Rome of **Gladiator** looks a lot cleaner than probably would have been the case though the streets are appropriately crowded. It was also a more violent city with murder, robbery and riots a routine part of life. Disease was prevalent, one consequence being a high infant mortality rate. Conspiracies were also common, often with a bloody aftermath.

The institution of Emperor was widely accepted at the time. Most Romans probably would have equated Republics with destructive civil wars. It is a modern (and particularly American) idea to think of a Republic, *ipso facto*, as a good thing. What the senators would have wanted is a voice in who was to be Emperor. The hereditary principle probably commanded support against the more risky alternative of people like over-mighty generals fighting for the throne. The plot of **Gladiator** in which Marcus Aurelius offers it to a general would have been a recipe for chaos, contrary to what the script has Marcus say.

In terms of general historical spirit, the film does do justice to several aspects of the worldview that would have been prevalent among real characters like Marcus Aurelius or the fictional Maximus. In particular, its emphasis on ideas like the importance of ancestors, family and duty seems accurate. Several characters in the film correctly refer to the importance of dying heroically. Given that death was such a close companion, how one died became much more important than in today's settled times. For similar reasons, stoical values were also cultivated and admired by many in that period.

The idea of loyalty to a good leader (e.g. Maximus to Marcus Aurelius) was widespread since the alternative would be perceived to be anarchy. Loyal followers would have been rewarded (though not with the Imperial throne!). Modern viewers might feel that the film's climax is rather corny (the dead body of Maximus being ceremonially lifted up) but it may well do justice to how real Romans would have felt. As a Stoic, however, Maximus probably would not have believed in life after death, a central plank of the film's narrative.

**NOTES:**

# Select Filmography / Bibliography

*Gladiator*, Ridley Scott (DreamWorks SKG, 2000).
The trailer can be viewed at http://www.gladiator-thefilm.com/

**See also the following epic movies:**

*Ben-Hur*, William Wyler (MGM, 1959).

*Cleopatra*, Joseph Mankiewicz (Twentieth Century Fox, 1963).

*Demetrius and the Gladiators*, Delmer Daves (Twentieth Century Fox, 1954).

*Fall of the Roman Empire*, Anthony Mann (Samuel Bronston Productions / Rank, 1964).

*El Cid*, Anthony Mann (Allied Artists/ Samuel Bronston Productions / Rank, 1961).

*Intolerance*, D. W. Griffith (Triangle Film Corporation, 1916).

*Spartacus*, Stanley Kubrick (Bryna productions, 1960).

*Troy*, Wolfgang Peterson (Warner Brothers, 2004).

## *Gladiator*, Ridley Scott and the epic genre

**Clarke, J**. (2002). *Virgin Film: Ridley Scott*. Virgin Books

**Coleman, K**. (2004). 'The Pedant Goes to Hollywood: The Role of the Academic Consultant'. In Winkler, M., ed. *Gladiator*. Blackwell Publishing.

**Cyrino, M**. (2004). 'Gladiator and Contemporary American Society'. In Winkler, M., ed. *Gladiator*. Blackwell Publishing.

**Ellwood, D**., ed. (2000). *The Movies as History*. Sutton Publishing.

**Hayward, S**. (1996). *Key Concepts in Cinema Studies*. Routledge.

**Jancovich, M**. (2004). 'Dwight McDonald and the Historical Epic'. In Tasker, Y., ed. *Action and Adventure Cinema*. Routledge.

**Katz, S**. and Jhally (1999). *Tough Guise*. Film with notes posted @ http://www.mediaed.org/videos/MediaGenderAndDiversity/ToughGuise.

**Kirk, J**. (2000). 'Sons of Hercules'. *Independent on Sunday*, 7 May 2000.

**Klawans, S**. (2000). 'Circus Minimus'. *The Nation*, 22 May 2000: 34-6.

**Kochberg, S**. (2003). 'Cinema as Institution'. In Nelmes, D., ed. *Introduction to Film Studies*. Routledge.

**Laski, B**. (2000). Interview with Ridley Scott. *Cinescape*, January/February. Posted at http://www.maximumcrowe.net/maxcrowe_gladpress.html.

**McAllister, M**. (2000). 'From Flick to Flack'. In Anderson R. and L. Strate. *Critical Studies in Media Commercialism*. OUP.

**McInnes, R**. (2003). *Action/Adventure Films: A Teacher's Guide*. Auteur.

**Macnab, G**. (2000). 'Lean Machines'. *Sight and Sound Mediawatch* 2000, pp. 2-5.

**Neale, S**. (2000). *Genre and Hollywood*. Routledge.

**Neale, S**., ed. (2002). *Genre and Contemporary Hollywood*. BFI.

**Nicastro, N**. (2000). 'Reanimating Rome'. *Archaeology*, July/August: 70-1.

**Provenzano, J**. (2000). 'Homo Maximus'. Posted @ http://www.planetout.com/popcornq/movienews/2000/05/05/gladiator.html.

**Redmond, S**. (2003). *Studying Blade Runner*. Auteur.

**Rushton, R**. (2001). 'Narrative and Spectacle in *Gladiator*'. *Cineaction*, 22 June 2001.

**Schwartz, R**. (2001). *The Films of Ridley Scott*. Praegar.

**Smith, S**. (2001). 'Beautiful Dust: Ridley Scott's *Gladiator* and the Spectacle of the Fine Arts': 35-43. Conference paper, Congress of the Americas, Cholula-Puebla, Mexico, 18 September 2001. Posted at http://66.102.11.104/search?q=cache:P_4n_vPp-WUJ:www.ipsonet.org/congress/5/papers_pdf/ss16.pdf+Beautiful+Dust%3B+Ridley+scott&hl=en.

**Solomon, J**. (2004). '*Gladiator*: From Screenplay to Screen'. In Winkler, M., ed. *Gladiator*. Blackwell Publishing.

**Stewart, C. et al**. (2001). *Media and Meaning: An Introduction*. BFI.

**NOTES:**

**Tudor, D.** (2002). 'Nation, Family and Violence in Gladiator'. *Jump Cut*, Fall, 45.

**White, B.** (2002). 'American Beauty, Gladiator, and new Imperial Humanitarianism'. *Global Media Journal*, Fall, 1(1).

Special mention must be made of *Gladiator: Film and History*, edited by **Martin Winkler** (Blackwell Publishing, 2004), a scholarly but very accessible volume, in which all the contributions are stimulating and informative, not least those by its editor.

Statistical information is, unless credited otherwise, taken from the Internet Movie Database (www.imdb.com/title/tt0172495).

Uncredited quotes from **Gladiator** crew and cast as well as quotes from fans are taken from various interviews and reports collated at http://www.maximumcrowe.net/maxcrowe_gladpress.html.

Several articles on the epic film in general and particular movies in the genre can be found at www.filmsite.org/epicsfilms.html.

Copies of the film script can be downloaded from http://www.starpulse.com/Movies/Gladiator/Script/).

For Franzoni's first draft, see http://hundland.com/scripts/Gladiator_FirstDraft.text.

There is a veritable legion of websites on the theme of **Gladiator**: fact or fiction. Some are by reputable historians, others by people who perhaps ought to get out more. An informative example of the former is by American historian Allen Ward which can be found @ http://ablemedia.com/ctcweb/showcase/wardgladiator1.html.

## Selected Reviews of Gladiator

**Bradshaw, P.** (2000). 'No Place Like Rome'. *The Guardian*, 12 May 2000.

**Brooks, X.** (2000). 'Fighting Fit'. *The Guardian*, 12 May 2000.

**Buckland, W.** (2003). 'Role of the Auteur in the Age of the Blockbuster'. In Stringer, J., ed. *Movie Blockbusters*. Routledge.

**Felperin, L.** (2000). 'Decline and Brawl'. *Sight and Sound*, June. Review and feature posted respectively at www.bfi.org.uk/sightandsound/2000_06/gladiator.html and www.bfi.org.uk/sightandsound/reviews/details.php?id=374.

**French, P.** (2000). 'Rome With a View'. *The Observer*, 14 May 2000.

**Hunt, N.** (2000). 'Gladiator Revives Classic Film Genre after 40 Year Absence'. *Middle East Times*. Posted at www.metimes.com/2K/issue2000-14/cultent/gladiator_revives_classic.htm.

**Knowles, D.** (2000). Review of **Gladiator**. Posted at www.aboutfilm.com/movies/g/gladiator.htm.

**Morris, M.** (2000). 'Empire Strikes Back'. *The Guardian*, 23 April 2000.

**O'Hehir, A.** (2000). Review of **Gladiator**. Posted at http://dir.salon.com/ent/movies/review/2000/05/05/gladiator/index.html.

A number of websites act as a gateway to large numbers of press reviews, notably http://www.metacritic.com/ and http://www.rottentomatoes.com/.

## Hollywood in the 1990s

**Abrams, N. et al.** (2001). *Studying Film.* Edward Arnold.

**Austin, T.** (2002). *Hollywood, Hype and Audiences.* Manchester University Press.

**Arroyo, J.**, ed. (2000). *Action/Spectacle Cinema.* BFI Sight and Sound Reader.

**Buscombe, E.** (2003). *Cinema Today.* Phaidon.

**Elsaesser, T.** and **W. Buckland** (2002). *Studying Contemporary American Film.* Arnold.

**Field, S.** (1994) *Four Screenplays.* Dell.

**Hauge, M.** (1989). *Writing Screenplays That Sell.* Elm Tree Books.

**King, G.** (2000). *Spectacular Narratives: Hollywood in the Age of the Blockbusters.* I. B. Tauris.

**King, G.** (2002). *New Hollywood Cinema.* I. B. Tauris.

**Maltby, R.** (2003). *Hollywood Cinema.* Blackwell Publishers.

**Miller, T. et al.** (2001). *Global Hollywood.* BFI.

**Shone, T.** (2004). *Blockbuster.* Simon & Schuster.

**Stringer, J.**, ed. (2003). *Movie Blockbusters.* Routledge.

**Tasker, Y.**, ed. (2004). *Action and Adventure Cinema.* Routledge.

**Thomas, A.** (2004). 'Anatomy of a Blockbuster'. *The Guardian*, 11 June 2004.

**Wasko, J.** (2003). *How Hollywood Works.* Sage.

**NOTES:**

# Bibliography

## Gender Representations and the 'Crisis of Masculinity'

**Beynon, J.** (2002). *Masculinities and Culture.* Open University Press.

**Bruzzi, S.** (1997). *Undressing Cinema: Clothing and Identity in the Movies.* Routledge.

**Butler, J.** (1990). *Gender Trouble: Feminism and the Subversion of Identity.* Routledge.

**Butler, T.** (1979). *Crucified Heroes: The Films of Sam Peckinpah.* Gordon Fraser.

**Fradley, M.** (2004). 'Masculinity, Masochism and White Male Paranoia'. In Tasker, Y. *Action and Adventure Cinema.* Routledge.

**Gauntlett, D.** (2002). *Media, Gender and Identity.* Routledge.

**Kimmel, M.** (1997). *Manhood in America: A Cultural History.* Free Press.

**Kirkham, P.** and **J. Thumim**, eds (1993). *You Tarzan: Masculinity, Movies and Men.* Lawrence & Wishart.

**Kirkham, P.** and **J. Thumim**, eds (1995). *Me Jane: Masculinity, Movies and Women.* Lawrence & Wishart.

**Lehman, P.**, ed. (2001). *Masculinity: Bodies, Movies, Culture.* Routledge.

**MacKinnon, K.** (2003). *Representing Men: Maleness and Masculinity in the Media.* Arnold.

**Mitchell, L. C.** (1996). *Westerns: Making the Man in Fiction and Film.* University of Chicago Press.

**Robinson, S.** (2000). *Marked Men: White Masculinity in Crisis.* Columbia University Press.

**Segal, L.** (1997). *Slow Motion: Changing Masculinities, Changing Men.* Virago.

**Tasker, Y.** (1993). *Spectacular Bodies: Gender, Genre and the Action Cinema.* Routledge.

**Woodward, K.**, ed. (1997). *Identity and Difference.* Sage.

## Society of the Spectacle

**Debord, G.** (1973). *Society of the Spectacle.* Black and Red. First published in 1967.

**Eco, U.** (1995). *Faith in Fakes: Travels in Hyperreality.* Minerva.

**Jameson, F.** (1991). *Postmodern, or, The Cultural Logic of Late Capitalism.* Verso.

**McKibben, B.** (1993). *The Age of Missing Information.* Plume.

**Mander, J.** (1978). *Four Arguments for the Elimination of Television.* Morrow.

**Mitroff, I.** and **W. Bennis** (1989). *The Unreality Industry.* OUP.

**Postman, N.** (1987). *Amusing Ourselves to Death.* Methuen.

The Peter Weir film **The Truman Show** (1998) has some interesting reflections on this theme.

## Pax Romana... Pax Americana

**Blum, W.** (2002). *Rogue State: A Guide to the World's Only Superpower.* Zed.

**Burbach, R.** and **J. Tarbell** (2004). *Imperial Overstretch: George W. Bush and the Hubris of Empire.* Zed Books.

**Chomsky, N.** (1992). *Year 501: The Conquest Continues.* Verso.

**Gelinas, J.** (2003). *Juggernaut Politics: Understanding Predatory Globalisation.* Zed Books.

**Pilger, J.** (2002). *New Rulers of the World.* Verso.

**Roy, A.** (2003). *The Ordinary Person's Guide to Empire.* Flamingo.

**Vidal, G.** (2002). *Perpetual War for Perpetual Peace: How We Got to Be So Hated, Causes of Conflict in the Last Empire.* Clairview Press.

**NOTES:**